Suzanne Stewart

DIVORCED!

A Key-Word Book
Word Books, Publisher
Waco, Texas

First Key-Word edition—October 1980

DIVORCED!

ISBN 0-8499-4128-8
Library of Congress Catalog Card Number: 73-22695
Printed in the United States of America

To

Sue, Sydney, and Hunt
for whom this story was lived
and written

Contents

Fear not, for you shall not be ashamed; be not confounded, for you shall not be made to blush....

For your true husband is your Maker, the Lord of hosts is His name, and the Holy One of Israel is your Redeemer; He shall be called the God of the whole earth.

For the Lord has called you when you were an outcast woman and grieved in spirit, and as a woman in youth who was rejected, says your God.

—*Isaiah 54:4-6*
The Modern Language Bible

I

That's the Way It Is

"YOU'LL NEVER SEE him again," the voice inside me insisted.

I didn't argue. The voice had been right too often for me to doubt. Shivering, I stood in the doorway as the solitary figure walked toward his car. My car, really. He'd asked me to trade for a few days—my Oldsmobile station wagon for his Buick Roadmaster.

He never looked back.

What do you think about when someone you love is leaving forever? What could I think about? It was John leaving. My husband. My children's father.

The light rain was clearly visible in the reflection of the street lights. He doesn't have his raincoat, I mused. Or overcoat, or hat. This is the first time in the years I've known him that he's been improperly dressed. His wool sports jacket will smell damp. The crease will come out of his trousers. This just isn't like him. Everything seems so strange. How can this man walking away from me be the one I know so well? His name is mine; he is not.

The lines of an old love song teased me:

> It rained when I found you,
> It rained when I lost you,
> That's why I'm so blue when it rains.

Not as dramatic as a Beethoven symphony, but a tune unforgettable now. No cheap sentiment for me. I'll just learn to laugh in the rain.

It was so silent. A wet world of chill and darkness.

The motor started. I closed the door and began the ritual of putting the children to bed. Hunt, not quite two years old, was the baby. The girls: Sydney, five, precocious and winsome; Sue, six, impulsive and beautiful. She asked many questions about her daddy. I answered matter-of-factly. We prayed together and kissed good-night.

I walked around the apartment touching things, thinking of homes we'd had in the past. Metal soldiers which John had painted stood on the mantle. I ran my fingers over the piano keys. On either side were vases that had been a wedding present. As a bride, I kept long-stemmed roses in them. The love seat had been our first piece of furniture. I snuggled against the arm of the blue velvet sofa John had designed.

Oh, Lord, is it going to be self-pity forever? How can I live through this night?

I pushed myself to the edge of the sofa and knelt. Tears began.

"Why don't you just enjoy it?" the quiet inner voice said gently.

The words surprised and shocked me. Finally I said,

You must know how I feel. My life is over! I'll never get over this! I'll never know another moment of love! How can I enjoy such a night? I'm dying.

"What have I promised you?"

You've promised to provide me with everything I need, one day at a time.

"Do you believe me?"

Yes, I believe You.

"Then live it. I have provided everything you need for tonight. Look around. See what there is to enjoy. You can choose to get through tonight any way you like, but it's possible to do it with joy. Don't choose pain."

I felt myself struggling. Which would it be? Despair? Depression?

I'd rather choose pleasure. Joy. Tonight, my talent for pretending would serve me.

Opening my eyes, I looked at the living room again. It really was pretty. French Empire furniture exquisitely upholstered. Hand-carved and hand-painted tables. A huge make-up case sat on one table. John had brought it earlier that evening.

Smiling, I opened it. Life really is funny. He brought presents right to the end. It was the main way he expressed feelings. Many of his gifts I'd treasured. Others I'd rejected. This, then, was to be the last. Oh, how awful to have let it go unnoticed while he was here!

The collection was extravagant. There were rows and rows of colors for skin, eyes, lips. I'd never had so many creams, brushes, and oils together before. Enough for a lifetime, I thought.

"Hardly, but it is enough to have fun with tonight," a voice said.

Silly, but the idea of playing with make-up was appealing.

Why not?

I had my Frank Sinatra records and my cosmetics. I

might as well enjoy them. I put on my prettiest negligee, added perfume, and started the music. I liked sitting on the floor on the deep pile rug. With the make-up mirror from the case on the table before me, cosmetics spread around, I began to make myself glamorous. Sinatra seemed to sing directly to me.

This is ridiculous, I thought. My whole life is a wreck, and I'm acting like a schoolgirl. I should be reading the Bible or doing something serious.

"Nobody need know," said the voice.

I smiled at the kindness and sighed.

Nobody cares either.

"*I* care," the voice answered.

I changed the records every half hour or so, remade my face several times, played and replayed one song. It was "The Last Dance."

At long last I said aloud, "Yes, it is."

I turned off the record player, taking one last look in the mirror. I was tired.

Two hot tears rolled slowly down my cheeks.

Good-night, Lord, and thank You.

2

Leaning

THE SEASONS AND I were changing. They would return at faithful intervals. I would never be the same. The winter of my personality had come. Tears would fill my eyes and overflow. Whoever said crying was a relief? It only brought more pain.

All I had were two checks John had given me the night before.

"These are good. You must pay the rent with the $150.00 one. The other will see you through a few days."

Nodding, I'd laid them aside as he warned, "Suzanne, I know you'd rather pay bills, but don't. First you have to have shelter, then food and utilities. You *must* be sure to pay your rent."

I tried to evaluate my situation calmly. Impossible. My husband was gone. I had two checks and a broken heart!

How could this have happened? We'd been so happy just months ago when our son was born. John visited the hospital the night before the predicted delivery date. It tickled me that he'd insisted they reserve a blue room. He lavished me with attention, and I bubbled with happiness.

My husband stayed late every night, holding me in his arms. Nurses were too kind to run him off. When he finally left, we had a good-night signal I could see through the window. John backed his car uphill in the hospital driveway, stopped, and blinked his headlights three times to say, "I love you." I responded by clicking my bedlight the same way.

Reminiscing wouldn't help. Responsibility for four people belonged to me and must be faced, like it or not. The man I'd married never faced realities. Now that our imaginary lives had fallen apart, I'd have to cope. If only I had a living father, I'd run to him! If only John's father were alive, we'd be all right. Reggie would have cared for us, just as my father would have.

Day after day passed and no one told me what to do. Mother had guided the first twenty years of my life. Now overwrought, she suffered herself. During marriage I had looked to John for authority. Now it was up to me.

I walked from room to room in the small apartment, feeling grateful for our furniture, clothes, and toys. The tangible things that remained comforted. Familiar possessions in an unfamiliar world.

The days were so long. Could it really be January? Time dragged as I waited for the girls to come in from school, and the hour when I could begin cooking dinner. I welcomed the few visitors I had. In Rosemary I found solace. Joyce cheered.

The three of us belonged to the Young Matrons Circle. For a fund raising project, we presented an annual Follies. I emceed the program. It seemed silly to be parading around in black fishnet stockings and a tu-tu just a few nights after being deserted, but no one asked about my husband. This surprised and perplexed me. Could gossip travel that fast in a city so large? Maybe it was that nobody missed him. Or cared.

I became anxious. Feeling panicky, I wanted to run. I felt alone in this crowd of happy socialites. Rosemary was putting make-up on the girls in the show, and I went in the dressing room to tell her I'd have to leave.

"What's the matter?" she asked quietly.

"I feel shaky inside. It's like a nightmare. Everyone out there seems to be so secure. I don't know what I'm doing here. I've got to go."

"Don't. I'll be through with this in a few minutes. Then you, Pete, and I can sit together." Her voice soothed me.

"Rosemary, are you absolutely certain Jesus is alive and loves us?" I whispered hoarsely.

"Yes," she said firmly, "and so are you."

Somewhat reassured, I remained, though not really able to relax. Even if I couldn't have fun in a ballroom with party people, it felt safe to be close to Rosemary and Pete.

Each day I tried to focus my mind on others. I walked to the backyard to watch old Mr. Dunlap plant bulbs and seeds. He and his wife lived in the terrace apartment. I marveled at his willingness to brave the cold and dampness, confident of the beauty that would spring forth in a few months with returning heat. I wondered if either he or I would be there to see the flowers bloom. He was elderly, and I didn't know where next month's rent money would come from.

Passing by the garden brought me to the McDowell's. They had a nine-year-old son, Mike, who always wore a football helmet. He was subject to sudden falls due to a disease which caused him to lose consciousness without warning. His mother was patient and kind, his father was good-humored. Mike behaved like a normal, outgoing boy.

I liked the whole family. They expressed contentment, love, and courage to face life's inequities.

My next-door neighbor gave a party one night. My

children slept undisturbed, but the sounds of gaity kept me awake. Next time I saw Eric, I mentioned it.

"Gee, Eric, I wish you'd invited me to your celebration the other night."

"It just happened. I went to a wedding and invited everybody I knew at the reception to come on over."

"My goodness. Were the bride and groom relatives of yours?"

"She was my fiance. I introduced her to a good friend."

"I'm sorry, Eric."

Sad. Everyone had troubles.

Life continued. The people around helped me by their ordinary living when I wanted to die. If they could live, so could I. The children had lost their father. It was unthinkable that they should lose both parents.

I'd have to be strong. But how?

Faith. Faith in a God of power. He could see us through. He would.

I continued to live one day at a time, struggling to believe He'd provide.

On Sunday we attended services at the church. My minister, Dr. Broyles, took me aside and said, "What are you going to do?"

He looked so serious and worried that I attempted levity, "I don't know. Can you support us?"

"No."

Then I thought seriously. I really wished the church supported widows and orphans. It was awfully hard to bear a heartbreak alone while others reminded you of practical necessities. I didn't know what to do about either.

Dr. Broyles had referred me to a lawyer, Jack Etheridge, months before when John and I had moved out of our home to separate apartments. Dr. Broyles thought I needed legal advice. I did consult Jack, but would not take legal action against John for separate maintenance or divorce.

Now Dr. Broyles said, "John is gone, Suzanne. You must accept that. Go see Jack tomorrow."

"Dr. Broyles, should I get a divorce?"

"A divorce is just a piece of paper to clean up the mess. What's happened has long since happened."

The next day, thoroughly humiliated, I sought Jack's help. I'd never given him permission to follow the legal steps recommended. Now what could he do?

"Suzanne, you're in a bad spot! John has left the state. It will be almost impossible to get support from him. Of course you can get a divorce anytime you want it. We have his signature waiving right to service of papers."

"I don't want a divorce, Jack."

"You'll be married again in two years, Suzanne."

We sat in silence for awhile. No need to rehash the old argument. Jack just couldn't understand how I felt. I'd gambled everything on the integrity of my husband, against the lawyer's advice.

"Jack, he still might come back."

Jack was quiet. He'd told me so many times the pattern men like John followed. So far his predictions had been accurate. What a fool I must be.

I wept.

"Oh, Jack, what in the world will I do?"

He sighed deeply. "I guess you'll have to go to work."

"Work?"

Startled, I realized he wasn't even aware of the love that constantly hurt me. I wanted to believe in John so badly. Work? That thought had never occurred to me. It was an obvious answer to the problem from Jack's point of view. It was something to think about. I could try. Relieved, I laughed!

"Yes. I could go to work!"

That would be something to *do*! I had waited for a miracle. Now I could act. A tinge of excitement stirred me with a jolt. Something real had come in, and I struggled to recognize it. What was its name? Then I knew, like the poet who said, "If Winter comes, can Spring be far behind?"

I opened my soul and welcomed hope.

3

Looking Better—Feeling Social

THE SHRILLNESS OF a ringing telephone startled me. Nights were quiet after the children went to bed. Few persons called.

"Madame Suzanne, this is Arron, your hairdresser. Do you remember me? I've been out of town for several months."

"Of course, Arron, how are you?"

"Wonderful, just wonderful. And you?"

"I'm all right. I've moved from Sandy Springs, you know."

"Who has been doing your hair?" he asked.

"Nobody. It looks terrible. Much too long. I haven't been able to afford to take care of it. My husband is gone."

"Ah, yes, I heard. No matter. You must let me do your hair though, for old times' sake."

"Where are you working?"

"No place yet. I've just gotten back in town and haven't decided whom I want to be associated with. Many shops want me, of course."

"You ought to have your own salon. You are gifted. I've never known a more creative stylist."

"Yes. Well, I will go into my own business soon, but first I must build up a clientele. You can help me. I need a model to go with me to get a job. Will you let me take you?"

"Sort of like a theatrical audition?"

"Yes, and I will specify that your hair is always to be done gratis wherever I work!"

"Oh, Arron, you don't have to do that. I know what it's like to need a job! I'm looking for one, too."

"Nevertheless, Madame Suzanne, I will always do your hair free. You are the best advertisement an artist could have. People always notice you. They will ask you who did your hair, and when you tell them, many customers will come to me!"

Before the week ended, Arron had accepted a position and I looked marvelous. He meant what he'd said! His contract with the owner demanded percentage basis and commitment for my hair styling as his model.

I felt strangely ecstatic about having my own personal beautician. There had been a bitter feeling over the loss of things taken for granted. I missed more than could be admitted. This wonderful gift seemed a miracle from the One who numbers the hairs on our head. Most humbly, I thanked Him.

> *Father, I'm thrilled to know You care about my appearance. Looks are important to me, but I've thought that was vanity. You hate vanity. I'm slow to understand Your nature. Sending Arron to do my hair is the sweetest, most personal sign I've had that You love me. You are concerned about everything that concerns me! Thank You. Bless Arron. Prosper him. Let his generosity toward me be accepted as if unto Jesus.*

After Arron did my hair so beautifully, I felt obligated to accept invitations.

Rosemary, Pete, Joyce, Kent and I went to a dinner at the country club. The evening passed pleasantly, but I felt lonely. Later, when we were almost ready to leave, I heard a voice singing at the table behind me. Turning, I almost bumped heads with the man.

"Sounds good," I said. "Thought it was Tony Bennett."

Surprised, he stopped.

"Go on," I urged, "the lyrics are delightful."

Distracted, he obviously preferred getting acquainted. He introduced himself as Dan O'Conner, but I turned away embarrassed.

"What's the matter?" perceptive Rosemary asked.

"Oh, I'm so mad at myself. I spoke to a stranger, and he's been drinking. John used to get so aggravated with me for talking to people I didn't know. Now I've done it again, and this man may be a nuisance."

"Don't worry, we're leaving. Anyway, you didn't do anything wrong, no matter what John used to say."

Dan O'Conner continued trying to converse and stood when we rose to leave.

"I'd really like to see you again. Please give me your telephone number."

"I can't. We don't know each other."

He clutched Pete's arm, "Introduce us. Introduce us quick."

We all laughed as he shook hands with each of our party. We kept walking toward the exit, but he rushed around in front of me and walked backwards.

"Come on, please. Tell me your phone number. I've got to see you again."

"Watch out, you'll fall!" He was attracting attention to us, amusing and embarrassing me. I felt both foolish and flattered.

"I've already fallen—for you. Tell me your number."

"You wouldn't even remember it. You've been drinking."

"Oh, yes I will. I can remember it frontwards or backwards. Just tell me. I'll remember your name and number and a thousand things about you. Bet!"

This *was* fun. I told him the number and left the club happy. The years disappeared. I was a college girl again, flirting outrageously at the beginning of a new quarter. I hoped he'd be able to remember the number!

He did call the next day. Three weeks later he was still calling. We'd found out the facts about each other in telephone conversations, but I hadn't accepted his invitations. Finally one came that I could not refuse.

Dan explained, "I'm going to entertain some clients. They're nice people, and it's an important account. He's president of a bakery. My advertising company wants to renew the contract, and it's on shaky ground. He and his wife have accepted a dinner and theater invitation. We'll go to Hart's and talk a little about ideas for next year's ad campaign, then see *My Fair Lady*. Please come. I need someone to make it a foursome, and you'd be perfect."

The night came, cold and snowy. Dan was nervous when he called for me.

"We're to meet them at the restaurant. I wonder if this is going to turn to ice?"

"I don't know. It feels like sleet now."

"It might come down hard and ruin the roads. It might get worse."

I wondered why he worried. Weather had never bothered me.

"Listen," he said apprehensively, "it is ice. Hear it hit the windshield?"

"Yes."

"I'll bet it keeps on."

Playfully I answered, "It surely might."

"It could stop," he said seriously.

"There are no other possibilities." I smiled, but he didn't notice. "Tell me more about the people we're meeting, Dan."

He was as difficult to distract in a sober mood as when he'd been drinking. Arriving at the restaurant brought instant relief. The other couple was warm and friendly. I liked them immediately. Hopefully Dan would relax now.

The waitress asked for cocktail orders. Mrs. Bakery-President ordered a martini. I said, "Tomato juice, please, with lemon."

"That sounds good," the gracious lady said. "I'd like the same, instead of a martini."

Dan winced. Did he feel I'd made a *faux pas* by not ordering a drink?

I felt quite at ease with the couple. They were older, probably wiser, and altogether agreeable. Things went well until after-dinner coffee, though Dan seemed strained. He certainly wasn't the gay young man I'd met at the club.

Mr. Bakery-President addressed me. "What do you think is good advertising for bread, Mrs. Stewart?"

I thought for a moment. Dan was probably holding his breath.

"Frankly, the best slogan I've ever heard was 'I'd even go North for Southern bread!' "

Dan glared at me and said coldly, "We're talking about complete campaigns, Suzanne."

Why the put-down, I wondered. Was he so insecure that he feared a compliment to the competition? Poor

Dan. He was having a bad night. How uninteresting he'd become.

As we left, weather again became an issue. The other couple insisted on going to the theater in their own car in case of emergency. The streets were ice-covered now. Many drivers had put chains on their tires.

Dan constantly called my attention to the slow traffic. I asked him about his other accounts.

"Let's get a report on the weather." He ignored my question and turned on the car radio.

Arriving at the theater, I made one more effort, "Dan I'm so glad you invited me. The dinner was delicious, and I've wanted to see this show since it opened on Broadway. This is a real treat."

"I saw it in New York," he answered. "I hope this sleet stops."

He had begun to get on my nerves, and I was glad to sit in the dark enjoying the entertainment. Then Dan started leaning over and whispering.

"This girl can't touch Julie Andrews." "He's no match for Rex Harrison." "This is a funny line coming up." Which I missed while he was talking. I couldn't believe this was the man I'd thought so charming on first meeting. Aggravated, I wanted to pop him.

After the show, Mr. and Mrs. Bakery-President suggested we'd better not go anywhere else due to the hazardous driving conditions. Enthusiastically, I agreed. My patience had worn thin. They headed home in their car, and I was trapped with Dan again.

"Lucky you live right off Peachtree. No problem getting in your apartment. My driveway is very steep," he explained, "I don't know if I can get in my carport or not. Have you ever seen anything like this?"

I didn't have to answer. He didn't need a listener. He went on, "Snow tires wouldn't be practical. I've got chains in the garage. If it's frozen over tomorrow, I can put them on. That is, if I can get up the driveway."

He left the motor running while he took me to my door and said a hasty good-night.

I paid the baby-sitter, who, in contrast to Dan, wasn't the least disturbed about driving home. After seeing her off and looking in on the children, my thoughts became prayer dialogue.

Lord, that poor man! Thank heaven this night is over. I'll never get into something like that again. What a bore. How could he ruin such a delightful evening? I'll never go out with him again. He is pathetic. No wonder his wife divorced him. As for me, it serves me right. I shouldn't have accepted a date when I'm still legally married. No matter how hungry I get for good food and fun, I won't do that again! Forgive me.

The phone rang.

"I made it!" Dan sounded happy for the first time that night. "I made it up the driveway! Slid a little and had to start up again. Boy, it is terrible out there. No telling what it'll be like by morning. Baby, you bundle up and sleep tight."

"Thank you for letting me know, Dan. I'm glad you made it okay. Good-night."

Hypocrite. I should have said "Good-by!"

Lord, I'm not a very good judge of men. I give up the idea of remarriage. John was my choice. If my

best turned out so wrong, as this silly date did, I'm
through. You'll have to take care of me by Yourself.

I went to sleep.
Lonely.

4

Available

"UP OR DOWN?"

"The welfare department, please."

"Up or down?" The middle-aged elevator man seemed to enjoy my confusion.

"I, I—" Stammering, I looked over my shoulder for a directory.

"C'mon get in." I obeyed, relieved that he'd assumed responsibility. "Downstairs is where they go for hand-outs. Upstairs is where the big bosses is. You want to see Mr. Ellis. He's de big boss." He looked at me appreciatively and, satisfied with his conclusions, started up. He eyed me curiously, and I was too scared to speak.

"Now you go right through there," he gestured as the doors opened. "Jest tell 'em you wanna see Mr. Ellis."

"Thank you," I managed to whisper.

Following his instructions, I passed through a large outer office and then to a smaller one. A secretary asked me to be seated.

I dreaded another interview. The experiences of looking for a job had been horrible. I'd felt rejected and humiliated as I was turned down place after place. It was discouraging. My college degree in Drama didn't really prepare me for anything, and too few education courses disqualified me for teaching.

Friends thought my talents were in public relations. By selling more ads to our charity club publications than most members, I'd met many of the top executives in Atlanta. Why not cash in on these contacts now? But I just couldn't.

Others considered it a natural for me to go into advertising and sales. I cringed at the thought. It would be very different selling for your own security instead of a "worthy cause." No, the pressure of commercialism would be too much.

Vividly I remembered telling John about a new friend I'd made while soliciting for charity ads. The close rapport we'd established in a few minutes excited me. John's pride in my success made him a good listener.

"Did you get the ad?" he asked.

"No, but don't you see, I didn't want the man to buy one when he told me about his wife's illness."

"You didn't get the job done," John said matter-of-factly.

I'd been hurt by his callousness. Still it was a lesson I'd remember for years to come. Set the goal. Don't be distracted. *Get the job done.*

Ruefully I thought how hard it is to reach a goal that's not of your choosing. I didn't want to go to work at all. But if I had to, then I wanted to do some good in the world. I answered every ad that seemed to be a "helping" service.

My rationale for trying to sell cemetery lots was that I might be a comfort to the families. However, I learned that this business was comprised strictly of commissions on lots sold to people not now in need. The ones that bought hurriedly, after a death, were taken care of by the cemetery owners.

A department store interview for a position as a bridal

consultant had been going favorably. I was intrigued with the idea of directing wedding rehearsals and being in many churches. For the first time I felt confident of being offered the job. Then the interviewer explained some of the rush cases, often out of town, which necessitated the consultant's taking the gowns. Carrying such a heavy load required physical stamina.

"You're little but mighty, I'm sure," she said with a nervous chuckle.

The interview ended cordially, but she never called me.

My height ruled me out of modeling, too. The demand at present was for tall girls only.

It was a sad business, looking for a job. I didn't know it was possible to feel so useless.

Even a Chinese restaurant had turned me down as a hostess. The worst part was the owner's being indignant with me. I had thought it a simple job of handing out menus and showing people to a table. He gave me a lecture on how much the job involved, humbling me.

Everyone wanted experience! That I couldn't offer.

"Mr. Ellis will see you now," the secretary broke my reverie.

I followed her into his office dubiously. A gentleman stood and offered me a chair.

"What can I do for you, Mrs. Stewart?"

"I hope you'll be able to help me." Slowly I began to tell him the circumstances that had brought me there. He listened patiently, asking occasional questions.

I talked a long time. Then he asked, "So your husband's gone?"

I nodded.

"You have no income?"

"None I can be sure of. He's sent me small money orders each week, but I know he'll run out of cash soon.

Of course, I hope he'll continue sending us money, but I really can't count on it."

"And you want to go to work?"

"Yes, sir, I have to."

"Who's going to take care of your children?"

A flood of emotion was turned loose inside me. I struggled for composure as tears filled my eyes. There was a verse in the Bible that said the Lord was closer than hands or feet. I prayed He'd be closer than my tears! Swallowing hard and trying to pull back the tears before they passed my eyelashes, I answered, "I don't know. It will take some working out. The girls are in a very good school for half a day. I'll have to find a maid who can care for the baby. I may have to use a nursery school that furnishes transportation. We'll just have to work it out as best we can."

"Do you know anything about welfare work, Mrs. Stewart?"

"Just that you help people. I like that." I liked him, too, for changing the subject. Listening to him gave me a chance to get back my equilibrium.

"We help people who are eligible. There are many factors to be considered. You could call them rules and regulations. We have to check out the people who come here. This means investigating. It's hard on the welfare worker. You have to go in and out in all kinds of weather —rain, cold, whatever. If it's your day to go out, you have to follow the schedule. Do you think you could take that?"

"Yes, sir."

"The job requires a car."

"I have the Buick John left."

"It costs the government a lot to train people. The first few months you're learning the job. It's a loss if anyone quits. Do you feel sure you could stick it out long enough for it to be worth our while to train you?"

"Oh, yes. If I ever get to work, it will be a long, long time before I can quit!"

"Accuracy in each case is paramount. If you approve an applicant for assistance, or if you deny him, you must be right. You are subject to being called before a grand jury at any time to defend your actions."

I didn't say anything because I didn't know what he was talking about. It sounded oppressive.

After a long time Mr. Ellis said, "Mrs. Stewart, you might make a very good welfare worker. You'll have to go over to the Georgia Merit System and take a test. They'll mail you and me a copy of your grades. That's routine, as all our jobs are under the G.M.S. I'm sure you won't have any trouble with the exam. It takes a few weeks to get the results. Then we'll send you a telegram granting you the position. You'll report immediately on receipt of it."

"You mean I've got a job?"

"As soon as you go through these procedures. It may take several weeks—probably a month. Can you wait that long?"

"Oh, yes. I'm sure we'll. get along somehow. It will give me time to work out something for the children. I ought to move to a cheaper apartment, too."

Gratefully I shook his hand and left the office. I wondered if the same elevator would stop for me. It did. The strange little man who operated it looked at me expectantly.

"Guess what? I got the job! I'm going to work here"

"Say, that's swell," he sounded incredulous.

"Yes, in about a month I'll be back to stay. Thank you for helping me."

"Glad to." He grinned as we arrived at the street floor.

"Bye. See you soon."

The relief was tremendous! The blessed welfare department! Oh, I was glad to be through looking.

As soon as I got home, I called Angela. She had initially suggested I go there.

"I got it, Angela. I got the job with the welfare department!"

"Job? You dummy. I meant for you to go down there and get some money!"

5

Rock Bottom

"You *can't* MOVE down there!" Mother glared at me.

"Mom, I have to."

"Your children should be in their own home. Dr. Broyles told you not to leave it."

"What else could I have done? We couldn't afford to live in it. The only way I've been able to meet the mortgage payments is by renting it to those people."

"You wouldn't listen to anybody. It was a mistake."

Defensively I said, "Well, I don't see how. Now *this* apartment is too much for me, and its rent is less than the utilities were at the house! How in the world could I have made the mortgage payments?"

"Well, that's water over the dam. Now you're settled here, stay here!"

"Mom, I can't!" Why didn't she understand? "There is no way I can pay this rent on a welfare worker's salary."

"John will have to send you enough money to live decently."

"I hope he does, mom, but it would be foolish to count on anything from him."

"It's taken you long enough to wake up to that!"

My heart was beating fast. Now I was getting really mad. "He's broke, mom. If he could help, he would."

"You just keep on believing that. You'll be the laughingstock of the town. He isn't going to do anything for you."

"All the more reason for me to live on what I can earn then!" I screamed.

We were silent for awhile. Finally I spoke, trying to sound calm. "I've been reading the want-ads every day for weeks. This apartment sounded too good to be true. The rent is—"

"*Good*! The location is terrible," she interrupted. "The children would have no place to play. You just can't do it."

I looked at her with an aching heart. She was suffering just as much as I had when facing the problem.

"Things could be worse," I almost whispered. My throat was tight. I knew how gladly mother would rescue us if she could. Years before, I'd gone to New York and lived in a lower Eastside apartment until mother's first visit. She'd stayed at the Waldorf-Astoria, and I did too. One afternoon we'd taxied to my flat, and she would not get out of the car. One look was enough! Before leaving New York for home, she'd established me in a Park Avenue apartment, arranging to pay the rent herself. Now she was in a reduced financial condition or she'd save us. It hurt to see her proud chin tremble as she fought the inevitable.

"A man can't walk off and leave his wife and children in this condition."

"He's done it, mom. John's gone."

"You've got to get the court to find him."

I didn't answer.

"Your children have never known anything but the finest care. They are accustomed to a room of their own. How can you put them all together in one room?"

"Mom, you're the very one who taught me children adapt easily!"

"Not to a firetrap!"

She was right about that. The building was an old house that had been converted into apartments—one downstairs, two upstairs. The outside didn't look too bad at night—just very dark. Daylight exposed its sagging roof and paint-hungry frame. The stairway was drab. You had to guess what color it had once been: yellow, cream, tan? In the dim light it looked ghastly and smelled musty.

Entering the hallway of the apartment almost choked me. I couldn't see a window. Four rooms opened from the hall: two bedrooms of equal size, kitchen and living room much smaller. All but the kitchen had fireplaces, but who would dare strike a match to light one? The bathroom was ancient with linoleum flooring and a dark green window shade. The old bathtub stood on legs. I wondered if the children could get over the high sides without slipping. All the rooms had windows along the outside walls, I noticed gratefully, but no screens. How did you keep out flies in the summer?

I shuddered, remembering my first visit.

"It's done, mother. I have rented it."

Stubbornly she replied, "It isn't right."

"I know it's horrible. Really, I don't like it any better than you do. It's a bitter pill to swallow."

"It will be ten degrees hotter in the city. Your house stays so cool you don't even need air-conditioning most of the summer. You'll be eighteen miles from trees and surrounded by concrete."

"Just my own trees. It's close to a city park."

"No! It won't do for Sister, Sydney, and Hunt!"

In a quiet tone I pleaded for understanding, "I don't have any choice. The most important thing is staying together. If I hire a maid—and I'll have to—she'll get over half my take-home pay. The alternative? That is really unthinkable and unspeakable. It couldn't be God's will to separate us. I have to do anything, no matter how drastic, to make a home. I can't make out a balanced budget on my salary, even with an apartment that's one-fourth of my pay. The only way is to cut expenses to the minimum, earn what I can, and trust God to supply the rest."

Silently I prayed.

Please Lord, let her stop talking about it soon. I feel like I'm going to break down. Doesn't she realize how this is affecting me? I felt like dying when we had to leave our home. Now the thought of moving from this lovely apartment is killing me.

"Mom, look at me. It's just a temporary move. Dreariness doesn't have to be forever."

"How can you afford to move? You spent almost $1,000 when you moved from your house to this apartment."

"I used professional movers then, and had my draperies remade and carpets recut to size. This time it's going to be different. My friends have offered to move me!"

"Who?"

"Rosemary and Pete and Joyce and Kent. Kent will borrow a truck and Pete'll hire a custodian from his company. They'll handle all the big things. Rosemary, Joyce, and I will bring the clothes and smaller items in the cars."

The tension in my body seemed to paralyze my mind. I couldn't realize the battle had ended. Mother's abrupt turn from the apartment to the practical method of moving was indeed a victory. Bless her heart. My fall from financial security was a cruel blow for her. We had different ways of expressing hurt. With others, I appeared confident and calm. Alone, no bravado. Fear of the future gripped me. My anxieties poured out in prayer, often with tears. The drastic decisions I made were radical to my way of living. The thoughts of a new life made me tremble, but what purpose could be served in showing it?

Mom's courage came through in action. She worked hard to help in every way possible once she accepted the situation. On the memorable Saturday I moved, she kept the children at her house.

I laughed and cried while my friends worked cheerfully. The house looked more like a firetrap in daylight than at night. I noticed the peeling wallpaper as the men brought in furniture at my direction. The children can amuse themselves tracing back the layers of violet and rosebud patterns in their room, I thought. Then fear filled me: *what if the baby eats it?* My attention was quickly diverted by one crisis after another. How could the piano make it around the narrow turn at the head of the stairs? The sight of my beautiful, custom-made blue velvet sofa being carried up the stairs filled me with fear that it would be ruined. Kent sang or whistled "Old Man River" even as he and Pete hoisted each piece, "Tote that bar. Lift that bale." Thankfully they didn't drop anything.

Joyce's voice rippled with laughter, "I never saw so many pots and pans. I know you don't use all these for cooking. Hunt can play with them." She shoved them in the lower kitchen cabinets. The clatter and banging hurt me. I remembered the times they'd hung decoratively with copper bottoms shining brightly.

"Where shall I put the crystal and china?"

"Don't unpack it!" I swallowed hard as nostalgia swept over me. "I won't use it here for quite awhile." Never, I prayed. Dining had been such a happy ritual. What had

happened to the many persons who'd been our guests?
Why hadn't they come forward to help me? They said
they were Christians. They were members of churches.
They joined country clubs, too, a cynical side of me said.
Oh, hush, I told myself. Forget all that. There's too much
work to do to think of the past.

Kent placed the love seat. "Here, Suzy, now you can
pitch a little woo!"

I laughed at the thoughts that came!

Suddenly I felt a stabbing pain when Rosemary shoved
an armful of my beautiful clothes in a closet too small
for hangers to fit in normally. There was no rod because
the closet was too narrow. The hangers were placed on
nails driven in the back wall. How would my clothes
look after such a pressing? Oh, don't let them get torn if
any other nails or wood slivers are sticking out. How will
they smell? What was that odor I couldn't recognize?
Maybe it was age and mold. Would bugs be in that wall
and eat holes in the clothes? The black ruffled skirt of
a Balenciaga original seemed to wave at me gaily. It
reassured me and at the same time made me reflect.
Where would I wear it now?

The day was nightmarish. My strength depleted. Somehow everything became orderly. Beds were made, silver
put away, even pictures and mirrors hung. My friends,
having done almost all the work in high spirits, could get
back to their own responsibilities.

My mother brought the children over in the evening.
They were wildly curious. I held the baby in my arms
and said, "Wait, Sue, Sydney. Let me show you through."

The girls had already found the bedroom with their
beds and Hunts' crib. Obviously they were delighted with
the sharing arrangement as they chattered happily on
each discovery. Mother and I looked at each other with
relief. After awhile when the exploring slowed down,

she said practically, "Let's get your baths and you can see how the television works here. One show before bedtime."

My hopeful spirits sank. A moment I'd dreaded had come.

"Sister, Sydney, let me explain something to you. There's a nice old lady across the hall. Our bathroom is hers too. Whenever we go in, there are two doors to lock. The hooks on both are low enough for you to reach. You must be very sure to unhook them before you leave the bathroom. You mustn't lock her out."

They all stared at me. Mother looked incredulous.

Finally the long day ended. Mother stayed until the children were tucked in bed. Wearily I'd walked aimlessly from room to room, touching, looking. Sinking to my knees, exhausted, I prayed.

Oh, Lord. I don't see how I can stand it. Why has this happened? Is it because I didn't appreciate things before? Or because I insisted on having a beautiful home? John called me the princess who felt the pea under the mattress. Am I too particular? How can I help being the way I am? Please get me out of here as soon as You can. Please make me brave. Don't let the children see my cowardice. Keep us all safe and together, no matter how bad it is. And please, please don't let me go into hysterics.

Fatigued, I got into bed and turned out the light. In the darkness I saw something I'd never seen before. Chills ran through me.

Two gleaming eyes were staring at me from the floor.

A rat!

Ugh.

6

Pushed Pretty Hard

Car.
Lovett.
Concerts.
I stared at the three words I'd written.

Oh, Lord, help me pray this morning. You know I've always liked to sleep late. I feel almost paralyzed getting up at this hour. I want to talk to You, but it is hard to even think. I wish I could go back to bed. This living room is an iceberg!

Here is the list of the main things bothering me. The car: I don't know what to do. Should I sell my wedding ring to catch up the payments? Or just let the finance company take it?
The tuition at Lovett School: where will I get it? Oh, please provide the money for me to keep Sydney and Sue in Lovett! They must have a Christian education!
Music Club season tickets: I ordered them again this year. I couldn't give up my front row seats. You have to wait for someone to die to get them. But how will I pay? Please, tell me what to do about these problems.

Minutes passed.

I picked up the pencil, reached for the sheet of paper, and looked at the first word on it. I added an e to car.

"You should not worry about material things," the quiet voice within said. "I have promised to meet all your needs. Pray, Suzanne, that you will *care* more about others and their needs."

The pencil wavered momentarily. Then firmly I struck the two t's off Lovett.

"Pray that you will have more *love* for others—that My love will flow freely through you."

Deliberately I crossed through the t's at the end of concerts and added an n.

"Pray that you will have genuine *concern* for every person you meet today. Someone, perhaps many, will need the sympathy and understanding you can give."

Stunned, I thought: What does this mean? Nothing so specific had happened in my prayer life before. Surprised by such guidance, I sat thoughtfully for a while longer, then prepared for the day's work.

The office routine went well, and I made home visits in the afternoon. En route back to the welfare department, I stopped for a red light at a busy downtown intersection. Glancing in the rear view mirror, I saw a huge truck barreling toward me.

He won't hit me, I thought anxiously. He'll stop. Of course he'll stop. Daddy used to say truckers were the best drivers in the world. I wished the light would change.

Another look in the mirror terrified me. He wasn't slowing down. I accelerated to move forward, red light or not.

Vroom!

I felt the sudden impact and heat filled my body. Conscious first of the noise and extreme heat, I realized sweat was pouring off me as pain tingled in my back, arms, and neck. Rubbing my eyes and seeing red, I was furious. This was too stupid and unnecessary to believe. How could he not have seen me and stopped? My blood raced, and I trembled. Where were my sunglasses?

Lord, I'm really angry! This is the maddest I've ever been—and the hottest. Sunburn was never like this! That truck driver must be crazy drunk. What a mess this is. Oh, I'm furious. I could kill him.

"Say 'Thank you.'"

What? Oh, Father, that is wilder yet! How can I be thankful when I'm this hot and mad?

Tears were stinging my eyes. Trying to hold them back, I saw people rushing toward the car. Resentfully, gripping the steering wheel tighter, I condescended.

Okay. Thank You. I know I could have been hurt worse. Nothing's broken. This must be the driver staring so desperately through the window. Thank You he's not hurt. I'd like to scream at him. Help me if You don't want me to chew him out. Control me. I will try not to be hateful, but it won't be easy! It was an idiotic wreck!

"Are you hurt, lady?" a frightened young man was trying to open the locked door of the car. He's so thin, I thought, regaining composure. He surely didn't mean to do it.

"No, not really. I just feel like I'm on fire."

"Can you get out? We can go in that service station and get something cold."

"Thank you," I said sincerely as he helped me out. The thought of ice water helped immediately.

The driver talked wistfully and anxiously as we walked toward the station. Many people hovered around his truck. "This is my first long haul. I'll have to call my boss. Gee, I hope he don't fire me. My wife's expecting a baby any day now."

"Your first child?"

"Yeah. We're pretty excited."

I tried to concentrate on him but many others were talking, too. A policeman appeared and asked questions. He told me my car could still be driven though the frame might be cracked. I should have it checked. Through the glass window I saw men moving the vehicles out of the street.

The young man made phone calls and asked if I needed to call anyone. I thought of Jack, my lawyer.

After hearing the story, he gave me instructions. "Okay, Suzanne, I'll take care of the details with the truck company's insurance. You will have to go to a doctor."

"Jack, I've got to get back to work. I'm just shaken up and am so hot!"

"You'll need X-rays. I'd be remiss in my duty if I didn't insist. These are strange sorts of injuries. Something might turn up six months from now. If you started having headaches or blackouts, I'd blame myself. It's best to go to a good orthopedic man right away. There's no harm in being sure."

Finally I agreed. Then I listened as the driver gave the name of his company and the person to call regarding insurance coverage. I was thankful not to have to bother with all that.

I decided to drive on back to the office and put my papers away. The driver walked with me to my car.

"I sure am sorry I hit you, lady. Don't know what happened to me. I just plain didn't see you 'til it was too late. Didn't see the light either. Guess I was thinking too hard."

"Don't worry. No one knows why, but these things happen. I just hope your boss will be reasonable."

"Yeah. He didn't sound too bad over the phone. I sure appreciate your being so nice about all this. I know you feel awful. Did you ever find your sunglasses?"

"No, the filling station man looked for them in the car and everywhere, but they seem to have disappeared. It's peculiar. I'm sure I had them on when we collided. Oh, well."

Little things always matter so much to me, I thought with disgust. I must have worried everybody to death about the glasses. They were Claire McCardle originals. I'll never get any more like that. She doesn't design them anymore. *Things*! No wonder I lose them. They mean too much.

At the office I took smug pleasure in not telling anyone about the accident.

My mother once had her sables snatched from her shoulders when leaving a crowded store in New York City. She uttered no sound, and her companions never knew she suffered the loss. I asked her why she behaved in such an astonishing manner. She answered, "Why should I have upset anyone? If I'd cried out, the thief wouldn't have stopped or been caught. The furs were halfway down Broadway. My friends' afternoon or trip might have been spoiled if I'd brought it to their attention. Better to be quiet, don't you think?"

My controlled silence came from far lesser motives, unrelated to nobility or selflessness. Unknowingly then, I thought myself superior to my fellow workers. If a truck had hit one of them, they'd talk about it for days. They carried on about much lesser happenings as if they were the most important things in the world. Well, this wasn't the biggest thing that had ever happened to me, not by a longshot! It was just one more irritating thing in a long line of annoyances.

Reality of more inconvenience came to me that night. The General Motors Acceptance Corporation representative took my car because I was behind on the payments. Now I'd have to walk to the grocery store and Laundromat. It wouldn't be possible to carry loads of wash and a baby while holding two little girls' hands. I'd have to do it after they were asleep and come home while the clothes went through the washer and dryer. That meant three trips to get the job done. It wouldn't be easy. Mamie, the maid, would have to get the groceries when the girls were at school and she just had Hunt to manage. I began to think you have to be mighty smart to be poor.

Lord, how much tougher can it get? John hasn't sent a penny in weeks. Over half my take-home pay goes to Mamie. More to the Georgia Tech student's wife who drives the girls to school in the morning and brings Sue home. What's left doesn't begin to cover expenses. And now no car! How can I get Sydney home at noon? It all seems so impossible. I can't do anything about it now anyway. Please send some answers tomorrow. I love You. Good-night.

The next morning I felt refreshed and assured that the Lord would take care of us in the new circumstances. I felt free to call a friend who worked a few blocks away from my office building.

"Boyce? I wonder if you could lend me your car today at noon? I turned mine over to G.M.A.C. and need to get Sydney home from school on my lunch hour."

He asked about the details, and I told him about the wreck. He was relieved that I wasn't hurt.

"Suzanne, I believe if you fell in the mud, you'd get up smelling like a rose! Sure you can have the car. Anytime. I'll meet you at the garage."

As good as his word, he explained I could take the car in or out anytime for Sydney's daily transportation and my bi-weekly welfare visits! He was actually glad to help me!

This arrangement worked fine. My spirit of adventure made me relish the daily dash to get Sydney, take her home, and speed back to the office in record time. Changing lanes on the expressway was my idea of playing American roulette. It gave me a triumphant feeling to make it each day without accident, defying the laws of probability.

As the weeks passed, I found many good things in the new arrangement. Boyce kept his car full of gas and oil so I saved this expense I'd have with a car of my own. Actually, I made a little extra, for the welfare department reimbursed me for mileage.

In time, Jack called. The insurance company had sent a check for $1000. I paid the law firm and the doctor's bill and had enough left for the Lovett School tuition and the Atlanta Music Club concert series!

With the Lord, the light was always green.

Care.

Love.

Concern.

7

Out There Doing It

"They told you not to read your Bible anymore?" Joe's voice revealed his incredulous reaction.

"My supervisor called me to a meeting with her supervisor. They objected to my reading the Bible on the roof during coffee breaks. Their argument was that a welfare applicant might see me either reading or carrying the Bible. If denied public assistance, that person might claim prejudice. He could accuse me of rejecting him because I had different religious beliefs. The supervisors concluded it would be wiser not to flaunt the Bible, and under no circumstances involve myself with clients' faith or lack of it."

"That's ridiculous!"

"Be that as it may, they made the point rather strongly. I expect I'll spend my coffee breaks in the coffee shop from now on to keep peace."

"The supervisors don't give you any, that's for sure."

"I guess they have good intentions. Sometimes Mrs. Jerguson's behavior makes me question her motives. Sometimes I'm convinced she's trying to mold me into a good social worker. Other times I think she deliberately needles me."

"How?"

"She questions every decision I make. At least the cases I okay for assistance."

"Mrs. Jerguson's been around here for a long time. I guess she knows every second generation welfare family in the files personally, and hates them."

"But why, Joe? Why is she so judgmental? She pounded me mentally with 'You've got to go by the facts, not feelings!' "

"Probably she thinks you're too compassionate."

"She never comments on cases I deny—only those I approve. It's strange."

"Well, Jerguson's not going to like giving money to any of them. She came from the same background they do. You've got to admire her. Too proud to beg, she worked hard to get out of the dependent trap. She knows the kind of people who come here, understands their ways, inside and out. Many of them do lie and scheme to get money. You can see her point: if she worked and went to night school and really fought to pull herself up by the bootstraps, everybody should."

"That's what I'm doing, Joe. Pulling myself up by the bootstraps. It seems as if she'd like me."

"Probably does half the time. The other half she's too jealous. It's natural she'd resent you. You represent everything she wants, admires, and never will have."

"I don't understand."

"Everything came easy to you up to a point, didn't it?"

I nodded.

"You're cultured and have acquired good manners and poise easily. The way you walk, dress, and talk put you miles apart. She sees in you the lady she'd like to be."

I went back to my desk grateful for Joe. At least I was not alone. He cared and would pray about the situation, and he did have more insight than I.

Over many months, I received periodic increases in salary and a new title. The work never got easier, but I enjoyed the counselor-client relationship. It offered an excellent opportunity to really practice the faith I professed.

More of the employees were friendly. The receptionist in the Intake Division began giving me the clients who came from the farthest distance. This made it possible for me to take long drives for investigations. I often picked up my daughters and took them along. It was nice to be with them in the car, and they enjoyed ice cream cones while I went in the homes to visit.

The receptionist also often gave me what promised to be the most difficult applicants. She knew their unstable emotional and financial condition caused them to be angry, hostile, often abusive and vulgar. Some of the other social workers were likely to retaliate with impatience or temper.

"I know you'll be kind to them," she'd whisper as she handed me the case folder.

Once a woman yelled at me profanely for twenty minutes at the top of her voice before quieting down. My method was simple: I waited patiently until she was ready to stop. Then I began getting the forms filled out.

After we left the booth and she was gone, my supervisor screamed at me: "Why did you let her curse you like that? We could hear it all over the department. Who does she think she is? You don't have to put up with that. You should have thrown her out. I was about to come in and do it myself when she shut up. You're crazy to put up with that wild going on."

"She couldn't help it. They performed a lobotomy on her years ago."

Mrs. Jerguson stared at me a moment, shrugged and walked away. I realized she didn't know about the now outlawed brain operation. It left victims unstable emotionally—a curse, not a cure. I thanked God I'd heard the poor woman out. My investigation proved her need and eligibility.

It wasn't always possible to help the deserving. One man came in late on a Friday afternoon for the initial interview. I felt he was truly eligible on the basis of physical disability. Nevertheless, it was too late to get emergency aid.

"I'm sorry," I said. "If there were any way to get you money this afternoon, I would. Our bookkeeping department has closed its books for the day. There is no way to get a check at this hour. It's almost five. I promise you, though, that I'll attend to your case the first thing Monday morning and bring you a check."

"Lady, if you can't help me today, I promise you Monday will be too late."

His stooped shoulders revealed his despair. He seemed hardly to have strength or will to rise. Oh, how I longed to cry out an encouraging word as he dragged down the hall. I had never felt so helpless.

On Monday I rushed the papers through and drove to the apartment complex he'd given as an address. When there was no answer to my knock, I went next door.

"He ain't here. He went to the hospital," a sweaty woman told me.

"Which one?"

"Grady."

Of course. What a stupid question for me to ask. Where else would he go but to the city hospital? I felt a touch of panic, driving as fast as I dared.

It took ages, or so I thought, for the girl at information to look through the records in answer to my inquiry.

"He's dead," she said bluntly.

The failure I felt was unexplainable and something to learn to live with.

"Joe," I confided one morning, "when I came here to work, I thought no other woman in the world had been left alone with three children to support. Every day now I meet four or five mothers in the same boat, or worse."

"You don't know your Bible. First Corinthians 10:13. It's common to man, or should I say woman?" he smiled.

"That's the word: common. That's the difference. In low socio-economic groups it happens all the time. In my social class it didn't. I'd never known a man to walk off and leave his wife and children."

"I'll concede it's rare to happen with no divorce, alimony, and child support. Even so, they walk out on their God-given responsibility as fathers."

"Yes, that's true. But if they at least support the family, they don't seem so bad. Gentlemen do that at least. Except John. The educated, cultured men may not care as much about their children, even if they support them, as some of these fathers who run away and then come back when the family's on welfare assistance. No wonder they lie sometimes, pretending to leave while hiding out around the corner. It's the only way they can help the mother get money."

"Some of them leave permanently though, like your John."

I sighed thoughtfully. The Aid for Dependent Children budget was insufficient for a mother and children. I often compared it to my income. The irony was that if I stayed home and applied myself, not only would I be eligible, but I'd have more money than I did working and paying a maid to care for the children! No wonder it was almost impossible to motivate an ADC mother to go to work. I could understand.

Some days later I asked, "Joe, do you believe God has a plan for each of our lives?"

"Most certainly!"

We were comfortably silent a while. Then Joe asked, "What are you getting at?"

"Joe, I've learned a lot the past few months. These people on welfare usually help one another. No matter how poor, they share. They stick together. They neither condemn nor criticize each other—at least to an outsider. They have a fierce loyalty. Some of the finest people I've ever known are either on welfare or are neighbors of those who are. It's a minority that make a racket of getting money from the government. The majority are sincere people."

He waited expectantly for me to get to the point.

"Joe, it's not that way where I come from, at least as far as I know. My people don't help one another. None of my neighbors offered me comfort or practical help when our crisis came. They tried to buy our belongings cheap!"

"Is that so?"

"Yes. My next-door neighbor came over and said, 'I hear you're having financial problems? Wonder if you'd sell me your riding lawmower?' After I moved from our home to an apartment, only one neighbor, Nanette, ever even called me. Why isn't there more compassion and loyalty in my socio-economic group? Where were my people when I needed them?"

"It's funny. You still think of yourself as belonging to a society you've left."

"Yes, because I do. I was born to that culture, not this. My children were, too. Heritage isn't something to be taken lightly. If God had wanted us to be poor and ignorant, He could have arranged things differently. I was born to people who became educated—maybe too smart. Perhaps we were fortunate, selfish, and insensitive. But I want to know why no one helped me. Why, come to think of it, I never helped anybody. Surely others had heartaches and misfortunes? If I was once unfeeling or unable to help the people around me, thank God I'm not that way now!

"I want to live where God placed me—where I belong. I want to go home, Joe."

"Sounds like a good idea."

"It's an impossible idea."

"Not with God."

I looked straight into Joe's twinkling, friendly blue eyes. They were intent. He meant what he said.

I reflected on Joe. He worked in the tax department, was married, and had five children. Always in good humor, he called everyone by name. Yet he was, strangely, usually alone. Joe wasn't in my socio-economic group any more than my present neighbors and workers were. Joe lived on the south side of town, while I was from the north side. He knew less about the things that interested me than I did about the car motors he tinkered with as a hobby. I'd never even seen him wear a tie. What did Joe and I have in common?

Our faith in Jesus Christ as Lord and Savior! Even in this, we were different in expression. Joe always carried tracts that poked from his shirt pocket. Some days he spent his lunch hour two blocks away standing on a street corner in front of the city's largest department store handing out the Gospel literature. My faith was more private.

Maybe this was the answer to why "my people" didn't help me. Perhaps they never knew how desperately in need I'd been. If I had another chance, I'd know them better, on a deeper level of friendship, as I now knew Joe.

The difference in people, I concluded, wasn't in their being rich or poor, educated or uneducated, aristocratic or crude. Basic beliefs determined the difference! I'd been mistaken about "my people."

My people were Christians!

I stared at Joe. Could this man, who'd never known the advantages given me, live with more faith, love, and hope?

Yes!

Determinedly, I spoke. "You're right. With God's help, I will go home! I'm going to find the real Christians and be one. This time I won't waste my opportunities and privileges. I will love my neighbors because God put them there, and because we need each other. If they are not as they should be, I'll love them for their potential. And my children will grow up knowing the difference between people without learning as I've had to."

Joe laughed.

"What's funny?"

"Obviously the Lord is calling you. It sounds like clear missionary leading."

I saw the humor and grinned broadly.

"*My* missionary field: Northside Atlanta. Home!"

8

Introduction to Lettie

"MADAME SUZANNE, WE will find a new salon after this week."

"Oh, Arron, what's the trouble?" He had worked three places since contacting me in the winter. My brain and body ached. It annoyed me to have to tolerate his bad disposition.

"No trouble for me!" he spoke loudly, "The stupid receptionist has trouble. If she could schedule appointments properly, the stylists would be *most* grateful. I don't suppose she can tell time. My customers have had to wait twenty minutes for their shampoo! I won't put up with such inefficiency. My clientele deserve more consideration. I'm quitting!"

The quiet atmosphere of Antoine's disturbed me. It added to the tension. Other operators worked as if unable to hear the tirade. Customers appeared to ignore his outburst, although I suspected all listened intently. The tall, blonde receptionist walked toward Arron as if to speak. He glanced at her disdainfully, and she turned away.

"Arron, you ought to have your own salon." I spoke hurriedly. "I've always said that. Why don't you think it through, figure what you'd need, and work toward independence as a goal?"

He didn't answer. Pressing the advantage, I continued, "You've several loyal customers now. Perhaps one would be willing to back you. All that would be necessary for a bank loan is a co-signer. The bank could use the equipment as collateral. I believe you can get going on your own if you really want to!" Maybe I could relax now that he had food for thought.

"Do you really think I could make a go of it?"

"Yes!" I encouraged, "You couldn't miss. I know you're the best hair stylist in Atlanta. No doubt of that! You need to get established in a good locale like Sandy Springs."

"Sandy Springs, the Golden Ghetto?"

"Yes, almost every woman within a radius of ten miles has her hair done regularly. You'd build a large following in no time!"

"Maybe you're right."

The power of an idea! His mood changed from temperamental sarcasm to creative thinking. I listened with real interest as his imagination played.

"We'd call it *Arron's*, of course, and feature my French Cut. We'd let the Eiffel Tower make the 'A' on calling cards and stationery. It would be sensational. I'd hire someone to play the paino on certain occasions and have a festive air."

I marveled! The beauty salon now hummed with activity and conversations, the tense silence past. How Arron's mood affected the place. Wow!

Lord, if an idea could get to Arron to Sandy Springs, give me one. He talks as if he's already there!

The voice reminded me: I've told you to *believe* that the thing asked for has happened.

*That's right! I've asked. Now I must believe: You'll
take us home. Thank You!*

Isn't that amazing, I thought. I gave Arron an idea, and
he's caused me to realize a great spiritual truth.

My hair looked very pretty after the comb-out. Little
did I suspect how important this was to the Lord's plan.
For that night I was to meet a girl who wouldn't have
accepted a Christian witness from someone with unkempt
hair. She went to the beauty salon *twice* a week.

I arrived home weary. Oh, how good a hot bath would
feel to my aching body. Each step on the staircase seemed
harder to reach than the one before.

Mamie reported what the children had eaten for supper.
The telephone rang. Answering, I heard a cheerful, lilt-
ing voice.

"Suzanne, this is Joyce. Will you go see a friend with
me tonight?"

"I'm too tired to do anything, Joyce."

"This girl is someone you should meet. She's having
a very bad time. You could help if you'd just tell her your
story."

"What do you mean?"

"She's going to leave her husband. If she knew how
hard it's been for you to be alone, she might reconsider."

"Oh, Joyce, I don't know."

"Just come with me. I know God will use you."

"I really can't tonight. I haven't had any supper, and
Mamie's about to leave. Maybe another time?"

"I'll bring your dinner on a tray. You can eat in the car.
Tell Mamie I'll pay her if she'll sit tonight. Please."

Lord, get me out of this.

"You helped Arron and now you refuse to help another? Am I too tired to help you?" the inner voice replied.

Forgive me. I'll go.

I felt remorseful, especially since my joy at realizing the truth that had to come to me at Arron's. Whatever I needed to get home, the Lord would provide. I could see it! Surely I should be willing to help another.

"Okay, Joyce. Come and get me."

As we rode, I prayed and ate while Joyce talked.

"Lettie and Rex were married to each other and divorced once before. Then they remarried. She says he's unfaithful and she'll divorce him again. Lettie will do it, too, unless a miracle happens."

"Well, my minister says infidelity is the one thing a woman can't live with."

"She can if the Lord wants her to," Joyce quietly assured.

Lord, how can I help this girl we're going to see? Please, tell me what to say to her.

Joyce stopped at an attractive brick house on a corner lot. I felt a pang of envy at the sight of the well-clipped shrubbery, grass, and a fenced-in backyard enclosing play equipment for children. A late-model blue Cadillac occupied the carport.

The door opened, and I saw Lettie for the first time. Her dark-haired beauty impressed me. I studied her unusual features—high cheekbones, slanted eyebrows, eyes that looked violet. Her lips were full and red against a magnolia white complexion. I thought she was lovely. She didn't waste any time getting to the point.

"I know why you've come, but it won't do any good. I told Joyce I'm leaving, and I mean it."

"But why, Lettie? You have such a wonderful home here for your children. How can you think of running away?"

"I've put up with Rex's behavior as long as I intend to! He thinks he can get away with anything and I can't do a thing 'cause I'm pregnant. I'll show him!" she said defiantly.

"But you've got to think of yourself and the health of the baby you're carrying. And the other children. You can't just walk off."

"Yes, I can!"

The three of us sat down. "How do you propose providing for yourself and three children?"

"He'll have to give me the money."

I almost laughed at her ignorance. "My dear, no man is going to fully support a family that leaves him."

"The court will make him."

"No, it won't. In the first place, they won't award that much. In the second, what if he skipped town? My husband did. I've never received help. A man has to *want* to provide for you."

"I'll make him."

"Wouldn't it be better to love him and be appreciative of his care?"

"*Love* him? After what he's done?"

"Why not? The Lord would forgive him. Shouldn't you? If I had a chance, I'd forgive my husband and work on being a better wife."

"I've been a good wife," she boasted.

"None of us are as good as we could be. Do you yell at him this way?"

"Well, I never!" she frowned.

"Perhaps before I'd have sympathized with you. Now

I know how hard it is to work all day and come home tired. I understand how men must feel. It certainly doesn't soothe or relax one to be screamed at with accusations."

"They're true!"

"Maybe. But if your husband is still here, he must love *you*."

"You don't understand," she protested again. "You don't see what he's doing. Look, I'll show you." She rushed from the room, and Joyce and I waited somewhat uncomfortably. When she reentered, an armful of shirts were dumped vehemently at my feet.

"Just look," she said triumphantly. "Lipstick on every one!"

Shocked, I tried to understand her. She seemed proud of her "proof," not deeply hurt as I'd have been.

Lord, how can I reach her? We're so different. She isn't my type at all. I'd die before acting as she acts. She's so loud. Irate. She makes herself ugly.

"Lettie," I spoke quietly, "it doesn't matter what he does."

"You must be crazy."

Lord, I'm getting tired of her rudeness. Please make her hush and listen.

"It's what *you* do that counts. God holds you responsible for *your* actions, not for his."

"God surely doesn't want a man to commit adultery! And I won't stand for it!"

"What Rex does is really his business, not yours. He'll have to answer to God, but *you're* not to judge or punish him. God will do that. You must be very sure *you're* in the Lord's will."

"You don't understand. He flaunts that woman in my face. I don't have to put up with that kind of treatment!"

"Who are you that your life should be perfect? No one else's is. You're spoiled and ungrateful." She looked violent.

Oh, me. I've gone too far. She may hit me.

"Well, I never! *He* commits adultery, and you think I'm at fault."

"Look at yourself in the mirror. You're in a fury. If this is the way you act before Joyce and me, how do you treat him? You seem mean as a snake."

"And what would *you* be like?" she yelled at me menacingly.

"I'd try to be a Christian. I'd thank God for giving me a husband. I'd be humble enough to behave better!"

"You'd let him go on with an affair?" she snarled contemptuously.

"Yes. If my Lord endured a cross for me!" my voice rose.

"Well, that might be all right for you, but it's not for me!" she shrieked.

Then impatiently I threatened, "You don't have to leave. Just keep acting like this and he'll leave you."

"Are you crazy?"

"No. My husband left, and believe me, I never acted as badly to him as you have to me."

The stillness was chilling. I longed to go home. My dingy apartment reflected peace, love and warmth. This atmosphere reverberated with the strident sounds of Lettie's voice making it a battlefield of anger, hostility, and hatred. My heart pounded. I detested scenes.

"He commits adultery and you want me to change!"

"You could rethink your attitude. You can't change

Rex's. At least not by ranting and raving, much less by leaving. Try loving him. That's what he married you for. He *needs* a wife to love him, not boss him."

Lettie didn't answer.

I sighed. "It's been a long day. We're all tired. We'd better go home, Joyce. I'm sorry about your trouble, Lettie, really sorry. I know it hurts. But I'd think a long time before I'd leave if I were you. Life is not easy alone, and your husband probably loves you more than you know. He's still here. I think you love him too. Why don't you give your marriage another try? If talking to me will help, we can get together again sometime. Just be grateful. Thank God for all the good things about your life."

Joyce and I rose and started toward the door. Lettie regained her composure.

"I appreciate you coming. I still think *he's* wrong, though!"

Outside the door I said to Joyce, "Wow!"

"Nevertheless, you got through to her."

"You think so?"

"Yes. You'll live to see your testimony change her life and lots of others."

9

Thanksgiving

"DR. BROYLES, MAY I say a few words?" Lettie stood, facing our minister.

We were together at the traditional Thanksgiving Day service at my church. I'd invited Lettie because her husband and sons had taken a hunting holiday.

Our annual Thanksgiving service was unique. The main part of the service allowed time for members to testify individually. Emotions could be felt even before the first person rose to his feet to speak. An aura of anticipation was transmitted through the congregation like electricity.

Fresh fruits covered the altar, symbolizing the prosperity of our people and adding to the atmosphere. Baskets of food had been distributed to the poor days before. This fruit would be shared by our members at the end of the service. On no other day did we feel more of a church family.

A sense of excitement prevailed as Dr. Broyles turned the service over to the people. Mr. Reeves had been the first to speak every year as long as I could remember. He could not always be with us, I realized with a premonition of loss.

God had been good to our people. Hearts overflowed with gratitude as one after another spoke of His love.

Often sentimental, never maudlin. Then Lettie stood and asked if she could speak.

I looked at her in wonder. This lovely girl, who'd had few advantages educationally and culturally, possessed poise few could match. A white wool coat enhanced her dark beauty.

Dr. Broyles smiled, "Yes, young lady."

"I'm not a member here, but it wouldn't be right for me to stay silent."

I sensed the anticipation of the congregation, listening attentively, and felt apprehensive.

Oh, Lord, what will she say? Please don't let her embarrass me.

We were so different! Lettie voiced her domestic problems easily, even to strangers. I kept mine to myself as much as possible, sometimes denying unpleasant facts completely. I despised admitting that anyone I loved had flaws in his or her character. Lettie made no bones about her husband's infidelity. Both of us had suffered humiliation, but our reactions were as different as our personalities.

Our churches differed in atmosphere, too. Hers was friendly in a family sort of way. When I'd visited there, she had introduced me to some by saying, "This is my friend I told you about. Her husband walked off and left her with three little children! Did you ever? But the Lord's taken care of her!"

I shuddered, recalling such scenes. Her church family probably knew more about me than my own! Our church people appeared more reserved, friendly but less intimate. I'd be horrified if they knew the true wreckage of my life. I prized my luxury of privacy. Would it be possible for me to worship where "everybody knew my business"? I thought not.

Lettie spoke positively, "God has blessed me through this church. It means a lot to me."

Dr. Broyles and the congregation listened expectantly. I crossed my fingers—not knowing what to expect!

"I'm especially grateful to the Lord for sending one of your members into my life a few months ago. At the time, I planned to leave my husband as soon as our baby was born. You can imagine how miserable and upset I was. She made me see things from God's point of view. If it hadn't been for her, my marriage would be ended. Now I'm learning to love my husband and accept him. I'm going to concentrate on doing the Lord's will in my life and let Him work out our problems."

Conscience smote me! I hadn't even wanted to go see her that first night with Joyce. Many times during our talks since I'd been bored and frustrated going over the same things. How her words shamed me! Imagine her giving me public credit for doing something I'd so little heart to do. I wondered why I'd been so sure she shouldn't leave Rex? Was it just the financial aspect? She had come to see the practical difference in her circumstances and mine. God blessed her and met financial needs through her husband, a good provider. No, I'd come to believe Rex and Lettie loved each other. I remembered my first meeting with him.

The twentieth anniversary premiere of *Gone with the Wind* had been long sold out when Lettie heard me say I'd love to go. She couldn't understand my attraction to a movie I'd already seen many times.

"It's not just the movie, Lettie," I'd explained. "I want to see the celebrities coming—Vivien Leigh, Olivia de-Haviland, and others. I love the entertainment world. I'd like to be there on the front row!"

She hadn't said much, but obviously such things had little or no appeal for her. Two days later she called me. "Guess what we're going to do?"

"What?"

"We're going to that *Gone with the Wind* anniversary thing you wanted to see."

"Lettie!" I cried. "How?"

"I read the want ads and found someone who had two front-row seats for sale!"

She'd paid twenty-five dollars for them!

The night lived up to my expectations. The beautiful actresses inspired me with their gracious, lovely personalities. Close enough to touch! Lettie could hardly realize what she'd done for my spirit.

When we left the theater, her husband met us out front, and invited us for a late supper. As we followed him to the restaurant, Lettie spoke angrily.

"See. He's checking up on me. Just making sure I told him the truth about where I was going and with whom!"

"But, Lettie, that's wonderful! It shows he loves you. I wish someone cared enough about me to wait outside a theater at midnight!"

Her anger, quickly ignited, subsided as she looked at it from my point of view. That was the story of our friendship—the differences between us helping each other.

I came back to the reality of the Thanksgiving service as Lettie continued, "I've learned so much in the Bible class taught here. I appreciate this church sponsoring it. Dr. Gutzke is the best Bible teacher I've ever heard. He has shown me so much! I'm grateful for him and all this church does through its members, and work in the name of Jesus Christ."

As she stood beside me, I thought of the many Monday nights that we'd attended the Bible classes together. Dr. Gutzke's insights enlightened and strengthened me, too. Funny, the same lessons that moved me to assurance that I should return to my home in Sandy Springs had led Lettie to stay with her husband! Amazing. It took courage and faith for both of us to do as we were led.

We'd studied the Patriarchs in Genesis and the Exodus and had likened ourselves to God's ancient people. Lettie and I were convinced: He loves. He cares. As God guided, protected, and honored Abraham, Isaac, Jacob, Joseph, Moses, and Joshua, so He would do the same for us. Of course, living it out presented problems because of our own weaknesses.

"And I'm grateful for you, Dr. Broyles. I know how much you mean to my friend. I feel like I know you and love you, too."

She sat down, and I pressed her hand in affection. How proud I was of her!

I listened to other testimonies. Many gave voice to the Lord's mercy and kindness. My thoughts flashed back a year to when I'd come to this same service with the children. At that time I'd been estranged from my mother and separated from my husband. Quite alone. I'd taken the children to a hotel afterward for dinner. Suffering a migraine headache, I couldn't eat. Facing an uncertain future, I was tense, apprehensive, and very lonely.

This year my life showed so many changes. I knew positively that we were in the Lord's hands. I was thankful for a job, a home, friends, good health, reconciliation with my mother, and hope! After church, my mother would serve us a marvelous dinner. I could count on love, peace, and joy at her house today. Then I'd take Lettie and the children out to *my* house: a home regained! The renters had moved out of my home, and my landlady had informed me she was selling the old house. With the timing of the two events, I felt it was a "sign" from the Lord saying "Go." It would be a leap of faith.

I wanted to stand and testify. My heart felt like bursting with the abundantly rich emotions hidden there. I couldn't trust myself to speak. Surely God understood.

At the end of that happy day, Lettie kissed me good-by, exclaiming, "This has been the best Thanksgiving Day I've ever spent. I couldn't be happier."

She could be though, and was. A few hours later a daughter was born to her.

IO

Wiped Out

I GLOATED!

Standing in the doorway, looking down the hill that was my front yard, I beamed.

Home! I'm home. I'm in it, and John will have to make the mortgage payments, like it or not. He's too good a businessman to lose such a valuable piece of property with so much already invested in it.

"Stop daydreaming and get to work!" my mother interrupted. "We've got to get busy on the floors. Those people left things in terrible condition."

Mother organized each of us, even the baby, and we scrubbed every free moment for the next two weeks. Not one inch of woodwork could get by her inspection unless it was spotless. Mary, the live-in maid I'd hired to replace Mamie, diligently polished silver and brass to mother's satisfaction. The dining room chandelier sparkled like diamonds.

By Friday, December 9th, I was worn to a frazzle. Getting to and from the welfare department was quite a task from this distance, and housework in the evenings had taken its toll. I planned to sleep as much as possible over the weekend. As soon as Mary left for her weekend off, I helped the children bathe and get to bed.

Father, I'm so tired. Forgive me for not reading the Bible tonight. I've got to go to sleep. Will You do something special for me? I'm ashamed to ask after all You've done. Would You make Your Son very real to me again? He was so close to me at first, when I realized He is living. Now He seems far away, almost a memory. Please. I need to know His closeness.

I fell asleep quickly, but the telephone soon disturbed me.

"Suzanne?"

"Oh, mother, what do you want? I'm asleep," I said crossly.

"There's no reason to be so ill-tempered. You're probably the only adult in Atlanta to be in bed before 9:00 P.M. on a Friday night!"

Later, another call disturbed me. As quickly as possible, I hung up and slept again. Then little Sue came in the room and stood by my bed.

"Mama, the blanket's too hot."

"Oh, Sister. I told you last night not to turn it on so high. You must leave the control alone after I tuck you in."

"Are you coming to fix it, mama?"

"No. Just slip in here. You can spend the night with me this time."

Things were quiet and I was almost asleep again when she said, "Mama, I keep hearing Hunt cough. Do you hear him?"

I strained. "Yes, I'll see about him."

Half-asleep, I stumbled down the hall. I entered Sue's room to turn off the blanket and smelled smoke. No wonder Hunt was coughing. His crib was in her room. Opening the windows for air, I saw a scorched place on

Sue's blanket. I'll have to throw that away tomorrow, I thought.

Gently I lifted Hunt, hoping he wouldn't awaken, and carried him to the other end of the house and placed him in my bed with Sue.

"Is Hunt going to stay here, mommy?" she asked, surprised.

"Yes. I'll get in bed with Sydney. Good-night now."

Sydney didn't stir when I slipped between the covers. I slept in exhaustion.

Hours passed.

Suddenly I was sitting upright, as if yanked forward. I coughed in pain, feeling choked, and squeezed my eyes. They seemed to burn, stinging as I opened them.

The room seemed filled with rows and rows of strange beings, going through the wall and up toward the sky as far as I could see. The beings seemed to be in two's, facing each other for a tug of war, silently wrestling with one another. The ghostlike figures were engaged in a war, I thought. They were fighting for my life.

Life!

My eyes opened wide. I awoke fully, leaping out of the bed. The room was filled with smoke. Instinctively I rushed out into the hall to Sue's room. When I opened the door, flames leaped out. I pulled it closed, badly frightened. Racing to the kitchen, I flung open the back door to breathe fresh air, my heart pounding. I dialed the only number I could think of. Nanette's husband answered.

"Pep, this is Suzanne. My house is on fire. Help me quick. Call the fire department. We've got to get out."

I ran through the hall calling to the children. I grabbed Hunt and pulled Sue by the hand, heading for the front door.

"Quick, Sister, take Hunt and run next door. Wake up

the Ellises. I'll be there in a moment. I've got to get Sydney."

The hall had filled with smoke now, and I could not see. Flames were at the end between Sue's room, the den, and kitchen. I headed through the smoke in the other direction.

"Sydney, wake up. Mama's coming, but I can't see. Talk. Answer me. Hold your arm out the door so I can find you."

Edging down the hall against the wall, I finally felt her small, soft hand. We rushed out the front door. The other end of the house looked like an inferno.

Outside, little Hunt shivered where I'd left him.

"Where's Sister?"

I pushed Sydney toward him, screaming *"Run!"* and started back in. Perhaps Sue had tried to go back for her little turtle. She'd just gotten it that afternoon. I cried out for her, but there was no answer. No sound except the terrifyingly loud crackling of burning. The flames filled the back hall now and blocked the door to the entrance hall.

Oh, God. I can't get back. If she's in there, I can't get to her. Oh, please save her.

I lifted Hunt's cold little body to mine, clutched Sydney's hand, and ran toward our neighbors on the right. There stood Sue! I almost fainted with relief.

Thank You, Father, thank You!

"Mama, they won't wake up."

"It's all right, Sister," my teeth chattered. "We'll go on to the Mooneys."

My bare feet hurt from running over the pine cones in

back yards and across graveled driveways. I glanced down and saw blood from scratches. I carried Hunt in my arms. Sue ran faster, ahead of us. Behind her, Sydney hurried along wearing her little teddy bear-like fur coat and black velvet shoes! Amazing, I thought. We're all in pajamas, the house is burning down, and Sydney had presence of mind to put on a coat and best shoes while she waited for me to come for her. Unbelievable! Then, wryly, I wished I'd snatched my mink.

Ora and Dan responded quickly to our frantic knock and call for help.

"Our house is on fire," I blurted.

"Oh, you poor dears. Come in. Dan, call for help."

"I called Pep. They're on the way, I'm sure."

Inside the Mooney's kitchen, I gratefully let her take charge of the children while I used the phone. I wanted John. Choking back a sob, I called his mother's house in New York.

"No," I heard her tell the operator, "Mr. Stewart is not here. He does not live here. I don't know where he is or can be reached. He travels. Is there a message?"

For some strange reason her evasive comments sobered and calmed me. How foolish to call him for help. He had left us.

I hung up and called my minister. "Dr. Broyles, I need you. My house is burning down."

"I'll be right there," he answered.

Then I called mother and Rosemary.

The kitchen was full of people by now. I could smell hot coffee. Fire engines had alarmed the neighborhood. People were streaming in. Even the Ellises were there explaining to everybody how they'd slept through our knocking.

Dr. Richmond spoke to me. "I've examined the children, Suzanne. They are all right. I think you'd better let me examine your lungs. You may have inhaled a lot of smoke."

"Thank you, Lea, I'm okay. But tell me, why didn't we suffocate?"

"Your system rebelled against the smoke. You may have come nearer strangling. I imagine choking awakened you."

The lady across the street whispered hoarsely, "Is there anything I can do, Suzanne?"

Her son had once thrown a rock at Sydney. I'd screamed at her then. "Yes," I shivered. "I'm so cold. If I had something to put around me."

She disappeared and returned with a pair of loafers for my feet and a lined raincoat.

I'd waited in the guest bedroom with the children who were in twin beds. With all my expensive lingerie, I'd been sleeping in mismatched pajamas of John's! Now, covered, I wanted to go outside and see what was happening.

"Children, come here." We all snuggled close on one bed. "God has been very good to us. Let's say a little prayer to thank Him. Then you can sleep a little longer."

"Mama, did our house burn down?" Sue asked.

"I don't know yet, honey. The firemen are trying to save it. Don't worry. God always takes care of us. This is a new adventure, that's all. You've all been so brave. I'm proud of you for not getting scared."

No one had shed a tear! I'd come the closest during that few minutes on the phone.

Our Father, thank You for loving us and saving our lives. We love each other so much and we love You, too.

I kissed each one, tucking Hunt in with Sue. "Go to sleep now."

I passed through the kitchen crowd unnoticed. Life is strange, I thought, as I walked back toward the house. My whole world is going up in flames and they're telling stories as if it's a party.

A crowd had gathered to watch the firemen at work. Peggy Yates stood on the periphery. Her husband carried our insurance. He made his way over to me.

"Oh, Alan, isn't this awful?" I gasped.

"It sure is," he paused, then continued resolutely. "Suzanne, you know John had the homeowner's policy changed to a rental property policy, don't you?"

I looked at him blankly.

"Your things aren't insured, Suzanne. Just the house— your furniture, clothes, and other belongings are no longer covered."

The arson inspector came up to me. "I'm Lieutenant Davis, Mrs. Stewart. It's routine to have an investigation —look for a cause," he explained courteously. I nodded. "Please tell me what happened."

I recalled the events in order, embarrassed at my stupidity. Guilt feelings plagued me as I remembered seeing the scorched blanket. Why hadn't I had the good sense to check it carefully?

Dawn arrived. Lieutenant Davis said the fire was under control.

"I'm going back to the Mooney's—second house down. I'll be there if you need me."

Ora Mooney met me at the door and said Dr. Broyles was waiting in the living room. I told him the story, and we sat together a long time in silence. The arson inspector entered, carrying the black charred remains of Sue's electric blanket control.

I introduced the men, all the while looking at the ugly thing in Lieutenant Davis's handkerchief.

"This was the cause, all right. A defective blanket. I'm sorry, Mrs. Stewart. Nobody knows why things like this have to happen."

After he left, Dr. Broyles asked, "What can I do to help?"

"I don't know."

"What are your plans?"

"I'll have to find another place to live. Maybe a furnished apartment."

"Have you any money?"

"No."

"Let me know what you need. The church stands ready to help in any way we can."

Mother was there by then. She took Hunt in her arms and said, "I'm taking him home with me! We're going to Rich's and buy my darling angel a coat."

She rushed out as if I might stop her.

Rosemary joined Dr. Broyles and me. We walked toward the home I loved. The firemen had done all they could do. The crowd had gone home. Daylight had come.

Most of the roof was destroyed. From the back, the middle of the house looked like a black cell. One side of Sue's room was gone.

"You'll have to have that boarded up," a fireman told me.

Dr. Broyles left us at the kitchen door, shaking his head. "You'll be at Rosemary's?" he called over his shoulder.

I nodded and waved. He kept shaking his head as if to say, "No. No. No. No!"

Rosemary and I cautiously stepped into the kitchen passing the burned-out area. All Sue's clothes, furniture, and baby treasures were gone. The prayer her godmother had cross-stitched and framed her first Christmas. The wardrobe Rich's gave her after she modeled in "Fashionata."

"Don't look, Suzanne. Let's just get what you need from your room."

We'd been told that it and the living room had only smoke and water damage. I opened my closet door. Sheer things fell apart in my hands.

"Rosemary, I think I'll die."

"*No!* God wants you to live. Let's pray and thank Him."

We knelt by my bed. The rug had been rolled up. It was lumpy and very, very wet. I tried to listen to what she said. I felt numb.

How long, Lord? How long will it take me to get back this time?

11

Sympathy

"What's wrong?" Rosemary asked, pouring me a cup of coffee.

"We could have died in the fire and it wouldn't have made any real difference at all," I murmured morbidly.

"No. That's not true," she spoke quietly.

"Yes, it is. You know it is. Oh, mother would suffer. You and Pete would be sad awhile. John would be relieved. He'd be free. Nobody else would care for long."

"Suzanne, God saved you and the children. You know He has a plan for each of you. Many people value your lives right now. You know the people in your church love you."

Why argue? She wouldn't believe anything else, and my feelings couldn't change. If I had to live and wanted to get along with others, I'd have to be willing to suppress such feelings. At least I couldn't express them verbally.

Lord, don't let me hurt people who want to help me.

In my depression, little things bothered me. There had been a gold pin clipped to one of the dresses we'd taken to the cleaners. The pin disappeared, and I noticed it immediately. The employees had no explanation for its being gone. I knew the lady who denied having seen the pin to be the same one who took the dress that morning. I was less troubled by the certain losses in the fire than by the apparent theft of the pin. I thought of it bitterly for days.

Rosemary's sweet disposition and patience helped me control my tongue. I couldn't be mean when she had opened her home to us. Nor did I want to show my nervousness.

Angela phoned. "Let me come get Sue. I'll take care of her until you get settled. You won't have to worry about her a bit."

"Thank you, Angela, but she has so many things to do next week."

"I'll get her to school and any place she's supposed to go. Let me help you this much. I can take care of her."

"She has rehearsals for the Christmas pageant. She's the angel." I was stalling for time, not wanting to be separated from Sue myself. I'd have to let her go though. Rosemary's house was small and it would relieve some strain on her.

"I'll get Sue there and to school, Sunday school, and anywhere she needs to be."

I drove Sue over myself in Rosemary's car. While getting her settled in Angela's beautiful guest room, Dorothy Connor came in. She had bought Sue a turtle the day of the fire.

"Oh, Mrs. Connor, guess what. My turtle got out of the house. A fireman told me he saw it creeping into the woods. Aren't you glad he escaped?"

Dorothy had generously brought a wardrobe of clothes to Sue. Her daughter, Patti, kept a closet full at both her home and her grandmother's. Sue would be well taken care of.

Back at Rosemary's, I implored other mothers of Sydney's classmates to include her in their car pool the next week.

On Sunday all of us were at church. Holding Hunt in my arms reassured me. After all, we had our lives!

Jack, my lawyer, stopped in the hall to talk about the fire. As he left he said, "Be sure to go back to work to-morrow. Best thing for you." I couldn't figure that! He always surprised me with his emphasis on work, but I took his advice.

Pete left for New York on business Sunday afternoon. Rosemary and I drove him to a hotel to catch a limousine for the airport. He got out of the car, then turned to speak to me through the car window.

"Suzanne, I'll be back in a week, but you mustn't feel rushed to leave. You are welcome to stay with Rosemary and me as long as you need. When I come back, I'll help you find a place to live, or help any way I can. Please know that you are welcome! Here's a little something you may need this week for incidentals."

It was an envelope containing five ten-dollar bills. I clutched it gratefully. How different Pete was from the man who lived two houses from me. After the fire he'd sent word through another neighbor that he'd be glad to let me have some cash if I needed it. There is such a difference between saying and doing! The man meant well, no doubt, and could probably afford to lend me money easier than Pete, but how could I ask?

Monday I worked undisturbed at my desk until Mrs. Lamb, the receptionist, came over and whispered, "I saw this in Saturday night's paper and wondered if it could be you?"

I looked at the bold print, "Mother Saves Three Children in Fire Here," and nodded.

"Your house really burned down Saturday morning? Oh, you poor dear. What are you doing?"

I explained briefly, and she went back to her work tearful and shaken with sympathy.

Word got around. A few people expressed their feelings to me, but little was discussed openly. Why did misfortune embarrass people? I wondered. Sad subjects seemed taboo.

The fourth day after the fire, Arron called to insist I come after work to have my hair done.

"Arron, I appreciate it, but there isn't time. I'm trying to find a place to live by this weekend."

"You will. This is only Tuesday. Come on to the shop tonight. You know you'll feel better after your hair's done."

He did not seem to realize the seriousness of my situation. Amused, I responded to his suggestion. I felt too much like a tragic figure. There was no point in looking like one!

Sitting under the dryer gave me a chance to review my situation. Relaxed, I made notes on things to do. Writing ideas on paper helped clarify my thoughts. I'd start toward the goal of getting the family under one roof by reading the want ads. Elementary, my dear Watson! Big problems simplified when broken down to the first step. I needed to put things in order, that's all. Everything would work out!

"You were right, of course, Arron. I do feel better. Lots better! Thank you for making me come out tonight."

"The spirit goes with the hair!" Arron triumphed. "Never forget, Madam Suzanne, you owe it to yourself and to others to always look your best!"

When I got back to Rosemary's, I found she had gone to bed with a cold.

*She's bearing the strain of my trouble, Lord. We're
a burden to her. Please heal her. I can't bear to see
her suffer and know it is my fault. She's so good!*

"Suzanne, John called twice. Your mother gave him
my number. He said he'd call back again."

So he knew! His mother must have told him. My aunt
had sent her a copy of the news article without comment.

The ringing telephone triggered my senses. An electri-
fying thrill of excitement started my pulses beating wildly.
What would John do to help? Would he come home?
Maybe he would take over the entire responsibility. Surely
he'd realize how desperately we needed him.

Oh, God, let him come get us.

"Hello."

"Suzanne? How are you?"

"I'm all right. How are you?"

"Fine. How are the babies? Are they all right?"

"Yes. They weren't hurt. We were very fortunate.
We're all okay."

"I'm sorry the house burned."

"Yes, me too." I swallowed hard and waited.

"I wish there was something I could do. This comes at
such a bad time."

"What do you mean?" I asked.

"Well, it's so near Christmas and all."

"Oh."

"I wish I were in a better position to help."

But you *can*, my heart cried. Aloud I said, "Don't
worry."

"It's such a bad time," he repeated.

"I guess there's no good time for a fire," I spoke dismally.

"No. Well, what are you going to do?"

"I don't know. Start over, I guess."

"I wish I could help."

"I wish you could, too."

"I'm really sorry."

"Forget it, John. We'll make out all right."

"I'll try to send something for Christmas."

"Thanks."

"Give the kids my love."

"Thanks for calling," I said mechanically. I hung up slowly, stunned with disbelief.

No help. He was no help. He was just sorry.

12

The Christmas Stranger

ONE WEEK LATER Mary, the maid, rejoined us in a furnished apartment right off the bus line. She began polishing smoke-stained treasures we'd rescued from the house. We were settled!

The children thought it was great. One more adventure, a new car pool, and plans for Christmas.

"Mama, will you get us a real big tree? I want one like we always have. It has to touch the ceiling. Mama, will you get it tonight?"

"I'm going to try."

"Promise you'll get it tonight," Sue pleaded.

"I can't promise for sure. I'm going to do my best, but it has to be the perfect tree. That may be hard to find."

My secret doubts hinged on getting a tree in and up! I'd never bought one before, but that part should be easy enough. For the first time in my life there was no man to carry it, and I hardly knew how to cope with that problem.

Lord, please provide. I'm not strong enough.

An hour or so later I walked along the rows of pines and spruces at a Christmas tree lot on Peachtree Road.

Cold air made my eyes and ears hurt. The attendant walking with me wore a hat with a bill that shielded his eyes from wind, ear muffs, a heavy jacket and dungarees, muffler and gloves. It was too dark to see anything but vaporized air as he exhaled.

"We must find a tall tree. The ceiling is over eleven feet tall. And it must have full branches. It means more to my children than anything about Christmas. The tree is very special."

After we found the right one, I added, "You'll have to deliver it. I have no way to get it home."

He hesitated. "Well, I don't know."

"Please. I'll pay extra. I only live around the corner at the light. The first apartment house past the filling station. It's not far. Please. My children are expecting it tonight."

"I guess I could bring it around on the truck when we close," he admitted reluctantly.

"Thank you! And could you bring a couple of boards to make a stand for it?"

To my relief, he agreed.

At home, Sue grinned broadly at the news. "Please, mama, let me stay up until he comes."

"No." I spoke firmly. "Sydney and Hunt are asleep, and you should be too. Tomorrow's a school day. Besides, we don't know when he'll come. It may be very late."

It wasn't. About 9:15 he arrived, saying they'd closed early because of the cold weather. I saw Sue peeping into the living room. I couldn't resist giving her permission to come in. She was so excited!

"This is my oldest little girl, Sue." I told him. "I don't know your name."

"We'll call him Tim, Mama, for *A Christmas Carol*,"

Sue decided before he could speak. We laughed as he took off his heavy clothing.

He bore no physical resemblance to the fictional Tiny Tim. Yet he wasn't the man I'd thought. Very young. Perhaps twenty-two. He had a handsome tanned face and an athlete's physique, broad shoulders and slim hips.

Sue pestered him with questions as he constructed a stand.

"Do you go to school, Tim?"

"Yes, the university."

"That's where my mother went. I'm in the second grade. What grade are you in?"

"I'm a senior."

"Where do you live?"

"Sandy Springs."

"That's where we live. I mean we did live. Our house burned down."

He looked at me for confirmation. I nodded.

"My daddy used to get big trees for our house, just like this one. We had one inside and outside. My daddy doesn't live with us anymore. He left us."

Tim glanced at me again. Embarrassed, I lowered my eyes to the newspaper on the sofa.

"Are you hungry, Tim? I'll fix you a sandwich." Sue went to the kitchen.

"This is their first Christmas away from their father. Our house burned down the ninth," I stated matter-of-factly.

"No wonder this tree's special," he muttered.

"Yes," I said simply.

Sue returned with a somewhat messy peanut butter and jelly sandwich, and a glass of milk.

"Thanks. That's swell," Tim told her. She beamed.

After a while the tree was upright, touching the ceiling.

"There. That's fixed good. You don't have to worry. It won't fall over."

"Oh, Tim, I love it," she clapped her hands. "The lights will make it so pretty."

"We'll do that tomorrow, Sister. Now go get in bed," I said.

The young man put on his coat, but shook his head as I extended my hand with fifteen dollars for him.

"No, ma'am, I couldn't take it. Not after all you've been through."

"But I expect to pay for the tree. Here."

"No. Ike's got plenty of trees. This one's on the house."

Surprised and pleased, I tried to accept it graciously. "Thank you, Tim. It's the prettiest tree in Atlanta, and we shall love it. I especially appreciate your putting it up. Thank you."

As I opened the door, Sue peeked around again and said, "Good-night, Tim, and Merry Christmas."

"Thanks, Sue, and thanks for that sandwich and milk. I'll come by tomorrow night and put the lights up for you."

He did, too!

What fun the second night. Sue and I both helped, thankful that Tim could reach to the top by standing on a chair. We had a good time decorating. The tree glittered beautifully when we finished and said good-by to Tim again.

The days rushed by. At work welfare people were applying for free toys. It was ironic. I wished the organizations set up to help provide them would give some to me.

I was called upstairs to the executive offices one morning. Wondering which case I'd goofed, I entered Mrs. Bailey's office.

"Mrs. Stewart, we know this has been a trying time

for you—a difficult month. We haven't said much, but most of us are aware of your personal difficulties."

I wondered what she was getting at.

"We—the entire staff—have watched you perform your duties admirably under strain. Customarily, we don't take up collections, as you know. This is an exception because we wanted to express our feelings in a tangible way. Please take this money with the sincere wishes of the staff that you and your children have a Merry Christmas."

Dazed, I accepted the envelope she handed me, murmuring thanks.

Oh, Father, I've been wrong about these people. They're not remote and unfeeling. This will buy toys for the children. Oh, thank You and bless each one who contributed.

Then I received a check from my Sunday school class. Many of the individuals in it had helped in various ways. Cooking dinner for me occasionally, baking cookies, bringing linens. They were dear!

Christmas Eve came and all work ceased. The children went to bed early and, surprisingly, went to sleep. Even Sue.

I began the first of many Christmas Eves spent alone. No one is guaranteed more solitude than a mother without a husband on Christmas Eve.

The doorbell startled me. Opening the door, I gasped.

There stood Tim, hardly recognizable—handsome, dressed up, obviously going someplace special. He thrust a package in my hand and said, "This is for you. Merry Christmas." Leaning over, he kissed me. Without another word he bolted down the steps and out.

What a remarkable young man, thinking of us tonight.

What had Sue told me? Oh yes, "Jesus sent Tim to us for Christmas."

Slowly I opened the present. A beautiful silver bracelet made of links that looked like pine cones. Deeply moved, I wiped away a tear. The Spirit of Christmas was very real. I read until time to put out the toys, then went to bed, glad for all the good in life.

Hours later the door bell awoke me. My heart pounded. It must be John! Surely he'd taken a late plane and would be loaded down with presents for all of us. Thrilled beyond description, I leaped out of bed, taking my hair out of pincurls. Frantically I pulled at the clips as the buzzer sounded. I had to brush my hair and fix my face a little. Trembling, I flung the door open.

My mother and aunt stood there saying gaily, "We've come to have Santa with the children."

Stunned, I backed into the room and let them pass. I felt the tears of disappointment, couldn't speak, and rushed back to bed hoping they'd think I was too sleepy to talk.

Safe in the dark, I tried to cope with the shock. How could they do such a thing? Wouldn't they know I'd think it was John? Their intentions were good, of course. They meant well. I could hear them giggling as they placed toys under the tree. One said, "I'll put on the coffee."

My body shivered. The bed was no longer a harbor of comfort or warmth. I shook with something like fear. It is so lonely when no one understands.

"Jesus loves me," I said over and over.

How do you know, I thought?

My arm reached out to the night table and I felt for the bracelet Tim had brought. Putting it on one wrist, I held it tight with my other hand. Holding something tangible which I had received as from God seemed to assure me of the truth in what I said. I repeated "Jesus loves me" until sleep came again that Christmas morning.

We cannot choose through whom His love will come.

13

Divorced

THE POOR BURNED-OUT house received no attention for months. It became an eyesore to the neighborhood and a heartache to me. I was powerless to bring influence on the insurance company. They dealt only with Mrs. Reginald Stewart, John's mother, the owner. They couldn't or wouldn't contract for rebuilding until she signed necessary papers, and she procrastinated until late winter.

I was up to my neck with financial problems. Somehow I met the rent every month, but pressures debilitated me. Neither the insurance company nor the Stewarts offered the money for rent to which I was entitled. This convinced me there would never be a reunion with John. He wouldn't return. I couldn't dream anymore. If he didn't help me now, why should I expect anything in the future?

"My help cometh from the Lord" the psalmist said, and I echoed, "Amen!"

Lord, You are going to see me through?

I felt an inner assurance, as if hearing a definite "Yes!"

Your wisdom will guide me?

"Yes."

Your strength will carry me?

"Yes."

Your courage will fill me?

"Yes."

Am I going home again when the house is rebuilt?

"Yes, but not the same way."

Pondering, I knew what should be different. My name.

I understand. Last time I hid behind a title that meant nothing. How false and cowardly of me to hang on to a name when the giver has gone. I am not really Mrs. John Sydney Stewart. I am Suzanne Johnson Stewart, and I'll make that legal. When I move back in the house, it will be in my rightful position as the mother and guardian of the children!

Convinced of the rightness of this decision, I called my lawyer. "Jack, I'm ready to get a divorce."

Telling him settled the matter. The responsibility for getting the job done was his now. And it seemed practical and convenient to do it while I worked in the building adjoining the courthouse. For a stirring in me suggested I wouldn't stay in the same job. I felt like a misfit. The drab surroundings depressed me. I longed for more beauty in my life. The only touches were the short periods of time I was outside.

Little did I realize the confidence I'd acquired after

only a year of employment. No longer insecure, the possibility of changing jobs held no terror. On days that I became unbearably frustrated, I'd take the afternoon off from annual leave and walk a short block to the Georgia Merit System. There I would have an interview and take tests for other positions in the state government. The scores surprised me when I received them.

Every time I scored in the eighties. Some tests were higher than the first one I'd taken for social work, some lower, but never more than two or three points. I concluded I was a "B" type person in any field.

Lord, I don't really want to work for the state. Probably I'd be as unhappy in one job as another. I will, though, if it's Your plan for my life. If a good job is offered me, I'll take it. But don't let an opening come up if You want me out of government.

It took a long time for me to muster up courage to investigate job possibilities in the religious field. I felt unsuitable and unworthy because of the mess I'd made of my own life. One day I asked a saleslady in the Presbyterian book store, "If a person wanted a job in a place like this, how would she go about getting it?" I didn't want a sales job, but the atmosphere intrigued me.

"Go through that door, down the hall, and ask directions to Dr. Walthall's office. He knows all the vacancies in the presbytery."

"Thank you."

Lord, I'll go see him another day. I'm not dressed well enough today.

"You're here today. Today is the day. Go on."

A few minutes later, trembling, I sat across from a handsome man with snow-white hair. This distinguished man was Dr. Walthall, and, by what seemed a miracle to me, he'd been immediately available. He listened, questioned, and advised me.

"We offer a service called Presbyterian Vocational Guidance. It is a testing and counseling program to help those deciding on a career. You don't seem to know what your real abilities are or the kind of work you'd enjoy. I suggest you call Mr. Charles Bovee and make an appointment. The fee is nominal, and I imagine he'd charge you less, say half, in your circumstances. You'll be better able to find a place to serve when you have a better knowledge of yourself."

I left his office encouraged and elated at the possibilities before me.

Lord, thank You. I feel You guiding my life. I believe You have something wonderful ahead for me. I will go as directed when the next step surely is from You.

In the mornings I walked with little Sue across Peachtree Street and let her go on alone to Carolyn's house. Carolyn, a teen-ager, drove Sue to and from school each day. The arrangement delighted my child who was naturally independent. "Mama, I can walk by myself. You don't have to go with me." She loved freedom. Filled with pride, I watched her. When she turned the corner, I waited for the bus to town. That is, on good days.

Bad days involved a crisis. Three separate problems had to be coped with each day. Every day three things could go wrong. Any one effected my getting to work. I depended on Carolyn for Sue's transportation, the car pool for Sydney, and a maid to care for Hunt.

One morning the maid failed to appear. I was filled with panic. If she didn't get there, I couldn't go to work. I'd lose a day's annual leave!

I let Sue walk alone and watched her fro.n the window.

Lord, please tell me what to do. Is Mary coming?

No answer, or else I was in too much turmoil to hear the quiet inner voice.

The bus will be here in a few minutes. Are You testing my faith? Do You want me to ask the lady downstairs to watch Sydney and Hunt and go on to work trusting Mary will come?

Still no answer. I was in a quandry. If I missed that bus, it would be impossible to get to town in less than two hours.

Oh, Lord, what will I do?

"Use your intelligence."

I tried to think logically, but it is difficult when you're upset. Struggling, I figured: The Lord hates sin. Being afraid is sinful when He has promised His care. He wants me to trust Him—certainly not do anything motivated by fear. He wouldn't want me to leave my children assuming Mary would come. Nor would He want me to impose on the lady downstairs. Why shouldn't I stay home with my own? I had annual leave for my own use. The majority of employees, I knew, usually called in sick, taking sick leave for personal problems and accumulating annual leave for vacations. They'd often made fun of me because

I would not do this. They thought my honesty proved
me a fool.

The decision made, peace filled me.

*Forgive me, Lord! Why do I wait so long to trust?
I should have thanked You in the beginning. No
circumstance is beyond Your control. If Mary is late,
or if I never hear from her again, it's because You
have a better plan in mind for the children. Emotionally, I'm retarded!*

Sydney's car pool came. I'd never been there before to
take her to it. I took Hunt's hand and we walked to
the driver's door. A lady lowered the window.

"I'm Sydney's mother. I wanted to thank you, Mrs.
Hertz, for driving her. Usually I'm on my way to work,
but the maid didn't come today," I explained.

"My name is Mrs. Walker. The Hertzs are on a trip.
I'm staying at their home with the children. Sydney
knows me. Is that your son?" she answered pleasantly.

"Yes, this is Hunt."

"How old is he? Three?"

"Yes, just last month."

"He stays with the maid all day?"

"Yes, until the girls come in from school. I have another daughter, Sue."

"You ought to send him to Fritz Orr."

I knew the Fritz Orr Club-Camp-School she referred
to. I'd sent John's younger sister there to camp when she
visited us in the summer. It was an ideal place for young-
sters in a beautiful locale, with horses, pool, and equipment for all sports. I'd heard the pre-school program was
excellent.

"Oh, I couldn't. He's just a baby, and besides I couldn't
afford it."

Lord, there I go being negative again.

Mrs. Walker wasn't. She said, "We have a nursery class for three-year-olds. I teach it. I'd like to have him in my group, and he looks like he'd enjoy being with other children. It would be better than being left with a maid all day.'"

My mind pictured Hunt with this kind lady. I imagined him riding the ponies, laughing and singing with other children, being comforted if he fell down. It would be wonderful if it were possible. But the money!

Reading my thoughts, Mrs. Walker said, "How much do you pay your maid?"

I told her.

"You wouldn't need one full-time if Hunt came to us. Why not hire one for the afternoons only. We furnish transportation, and Hunt wouldn't get home until after lunch. The difference in salary would pay his tuition, and you might even save five or ten dollars a week. Think about it!"

"I will. It's a glorious idea."

"Maybe it will work out for you. We'd love that little fellow!"

As she drove away, my heart pounded as I considered her suggestion. It seemed too good to be true. Million-aires' children went to Fritz Orr. Was it possible my son could attend? Could it be worked out with part-time help so I'd actually reduce my expenses? It didn't make sense! Send a child to private school and economize? Only God could arrange something that nice. I could hardly wait to start working it out. Expectation of good things excited me, and the thought of having three children in private schools tickled me!

*Lord, is this Your will? It seems too extra-ordinary
to be otherwise. I'm too excited to know, and I con-
fess it appeals to the snob in me.*

"Put out a fleece, as my servant Gideon did."

*Okay. If I never hear from Mary and can find a
suitable part-time maid, if the finances and transportation time works out right, if everything develops
smoothly and easily, I'll know it's from You.*

The prayer was answered, and Hunt matriculated at
Fritz Orr the next day.

One spring day Jack Etheridge called and asked me to
meet him at the courthouse at 10:00 A.M. Knowing what
it meant, I determined I'd play my last role as Mrs.
John Sydney Stewart the way my husband would have
liked it. Packing a small suitcase, I went to work as
usual. About 9:55 I changed clothes in the ladies' room
and rushed to meet Jack dressed to the hilt: mink stole,
kid gloves, and Mr. John hat.

Judge Virlyn Moore, Chief of the Superior Court, addressed me after I was sworn in.

"Young lady, you work here in the courthouse?" he
asked.

"In the connecting building."

"Well, you better get back to work. Mr. Etheridge and
I can finish this."

I left the witness stand, slipped off my finery, and returned to my desk. It had been barely fifteen minutes
since I'd left it.

No one suspected I'd been divorced on my coffee
break.

14

Faith Means Risk

"When are you moving back to your home? Surely it's been rebuilt by now?"

I parried such questions with a legitimate excuse. "Yes, the repairs have been completed, but I've decided to wait until school's out. The children have had to make so many adjustments with moving and car pools already."

Secretly I dreaded going back to Sandy Springs because of the personal physical hardship. Living close to the city made life easier for me, but I realized the children needed a home.

Joe listened to my troubles. As usual, I confided the difficulty of the situation.

"See, Joe, that couple of weeks we were in the house before the fire taught me a lesson. Before I moved in on blind faith. Now I know how tough it will be."

"Just what makes it so hard?" he asked.

"I had to get up so early, while it was dark, and walk about half a mile to catch a bus on Roswell Road at 6:55. After getting downtown, I still had a long walk, or run really, to get to my desk by 8:15. At the end of the day I could hardly run the seven blocks to catch the 5:20 bus home. When I missed it, I had to wait for the 6:10 which didn't get to Sandy Springs until after 7:00. Then I still had a long walk home. Being away from home over twelve hours with all that exercise exhausted me. You can imagine the extra trials in bad weather!"

Joe shook his head sympathetically, and I continued, "But that's not the worst part. Some days I hardly saw the girls and didn't see Hunt at all. Mary would have put him to bed before I got home. I could only slip in his room and kiss him as he lay asleep. Can you feature that? A mother not getting to hold her baby for a whole day?"

We sat in silence. I felt deep hurt, even bitterness, at being deprived of the right to be home with my children.

Finally Joe said, "Let's pray about it. If the Lord wants you to live there, He can make it easier."

"There's another big *if* too. I would need a live-in maid, and good ones are hard to find. I dread even trying to hire one."

A few nights later mother brought me a ray of hope.

"Suzanne, I don't want to interfere in your business, but an idea occurred to me."

"What is it, mom?"

"I met a charming young girl named Jenny. She's a student at the University of Georgia and plans to marry a student now at Emory. He's studying to be a doctor. Jenny would like a job in Atlanta this summer to be near him and save money for the future. The trouble is, she isn't qualified for office work. She really wants a simple job so she can take a correspondence course, getting college credit. She can't set up housekeeping in town for that would take all she could earn. I thought perhaps she might be interested in living at your house and acting as a nurse-companion for the children for room and board and a small salary."

"Mother, that's a wonderful idea! Do you think she'd do it?"

"I wanted to discuss it with you first. If you like, I'll talk to her about it now."

"Oh, yes, do! I think it's a great idea."

She promised to let me know something as soon as she could.

Days passed with no word. I felt pretty depressed as I entered the coffee shop one morning. Joe waved me over to his table.

"Joe, you always look so happy!"

"Any Christian should. We've got everything to be happy about."

"Yes, I know, but you put most of us to shame. Me, anyway. I'd give anything to feel and act as you do. I can't seem to get rid of this feeling of things going against me. Like Satchel Paige said, 'Don't look back. Something may be gaining on you.'"

"Who's Satchel Paige?"

"A baseball player."

"Forgive me for changing the subject, but our fifteen minutes goes by fast. I've got some news."

"What?" I asked expectantly. Joe was beaming with pleasure.

"My wife Bea and I have been talking and praying about you. We've got two cars—neither much good—but we only need one. We feel the Lord would like us to give you the other."

"Joe!" I exclaimed.

"That's my name," he grinned broadly.

"I don't know what to say. I've never heard of anything so generous."

"No need to say anything. We'll drive over Saturday to bring it to you. Maybe we can help you pack. You ought to be going back home soon."

A car would make that possible!

They came Saturday, as promised. Characteristically, they insisted on my having the better of the two cars—an old model Cadillac, still comfortable and really luxurious.

On Sunday afternoon more welcome visitors arrived. Mother brought Jenny and her parents to meet me. We discussed plans for the summer. The arrangement would benefit each of us. Jenny had a driver's license so I proposed she take me back and forth to the bus daily. Then she could keep the car to grocery shop and take the children to modeling jobs.

"Jobs?" Jenny's father asked, surprised.

"Yes," I smiled proudly, "Sue and Sydney 'went to work' when I did. They started modeling for Rich's when they were four and five. Now they get calls from several advertisers through an agent. I've had to turn many down because there was no one available to take them for fittings and jobs! The children's fashion coordinator at Rich's asked me to let Hunt start in a show when he turned three last February."

"Do they make much money?" Jenny questioned excitedly.

"No, not really, but I think it's grand experience for them. The girls enjoy the shows and like seeing their pictures occasionally. Often they get merchandise instead of cash, and that's like having a present to open when it's not birthday or Christmas time. They do make good money for television spots for advertising agencies, but those calls are rarer. They've made as much as $20 an hour, but even if it's just a slip and panties from Rich's, it actually helps us!"

Jenny exclaimed, "Oh, I'm going to like working for you!"

Her father smiled understandingly, "Yes, I think it will be a good experience for you to live with Mrs. Stewart."

"I'm so glad!" I said. "We really need Jenny. Let's

drive out to my house now so you can see where we'll be living."

My suggestion was accepted, and we piled into a car and drove toward home. Everyone chatted gaily, and I had to shout directions to Jenny's father.

"We turn here. That's the neighborhood swimming pool on the right. Each family in the neighborhood contributed to build it. We have a fine lifeguard staff. Down that path are the tennis courts. Now keep looking ahead. When we round the next corner, our house will be facing us."

The house looked beautiful. The lawn was still green though it hadn't been fertilized in a long time. I felt a surge of pride and confidence! The future would be better than the past!

Jenny's father eased the car to a stop in the driveway. I rushed ahead to open the door.

What a jolt! Excitedly I'd leaned forward to enter, but the door didn't budge. Instantly I felt deflated and afraid.

"That's strange. The key didn't work. Let me try the back door."

Did they all stand still or follow me around the house? Were they still chatting happily? I couldn't know because anxiety placed me in a world apart. I couldn't have been more alone. Sickness close to nausea almost overcame me as I glanced at each locked window. They were obviously fastened securely. The back door, too, failed to yield to my key. The deep sunken feeling had to be covered up. Brightly I spoke, hoping my explanation was sufficient, "I guess the workmen put new locks on. I'll have to get a new set of keys. I'm so sorry. I wanted you to see the inside. Especially Jenny's room."

They accepted my explanation, and we returned to the apartment. The children talked incessantly to Jenny, whom they'd taken to instantly. I tried to appear cheerful, but a forboding of disaster gripped me.

The next week school dismissed for the summer. The time had come to take action, ready or not. Despising any cowardice, I prayed earnestly for God's help, seeking promises of reassurance in the Bible. Finally I had the nerve to call Mrs. Stewart's lawyer.

"Be wise as a serpent," the inner voice cautioned.

"Hello, Mr. Pratt? This is Suzanne Stewart."

"Yes, how are you?"

"Just fine, thank you. How's the house coming along?"

"It's in the last stages. The workmen are moving right along."

"Good. Mr. Pratt, I want to congratulate you on getting it rebuilt. I know how difficult it is to do business with Mrs. Stewart. She's so negligent about answering mail."

"Yes, Mrs. Stewart is slow, but we have things under control."

"You must be very patient," I cooed. "May I ask you something personal?"

"Yes, of course," he sounded pleased.

"How do you ever expect to get paid for your work? You know John left many bills when he left town, neither he nor his mother send me money."

"Oh, that's easy! When the house is completed, I'll sell it, take my fee, and send Mrs. Stewart the difference," he boasted.

My heart pounded with anger, but I controlled my voice. "That is clever of you!" Indignantly, I remembered his call to me offering to pay the moving van if I could store my things somewhere. He had assured me he would pay for it to be returned when I moved back!

"Only way to do business with her."

"Well, best wishes, Mr. Pratt. It was nice to talk with you."

"Hope all goes well with you, too, Mrs. Stewart. Good-by."

I wanted to scream. Shaking, I fought the impulse to burst forth in a tirade. Instead, I rushed into the ladies' room, and threw cold water on my face, fighting tears of indignation.

Oh, God, help me. You surely don't want it to be this way. Should my children have no home because of the greed of these people? I've been so patient with John and his mother. I've forgiven them and forgiven them, but this is too much. That man will sell our home and take the money!

"Not unless you let him."

I stopped splashing water and stood perfectly still.

What can I do?

"Simple. Move in."

I tried to think. An old adage came to mind. "Possession is nine-tenths of the law" or something like that. Yes, I thought, who would dare try to throw us out? They couldn't sell it with us living there. I wouldn't let anyone in to see it! Exciting but unpleasant thrills replaced the fear. I had suppressed emotions for so long that exhilaration seemed a treat.

Lord, You know I don't want to fight. I've tried to live in peace with the Stewarts, but I'm not able to let them take the house.

"For everything there is a season . . . a time for war, and a time for peace."

I understand. This is war. No one else cares about my children. If they are to have a home, I must be willing to fight for it. And I am. You promised Joshua You'd be with him in battle—that every step he trod would become his possession.

"Be strong and of good courage. . . . It is the Lord who goes before you; he will be with you . . . do not fear or be dismayed."

Quite deliberately, then, I planned my move. From somewhere, I remembered that you must take an enemy by surprise. I'd move in now, whether the house was finished or not. Quickly. Before Mr. Pratt could suspect anything.

I'd break in.

15

The Rape of the Lock

I REALLY DIDN'T want any witnesses to my break-in. Repairmen worked at the house during the week, so a Saturday attack seemed to lessen the chances of confrontation. That was the day to move. But I'd have to arrive before the movers brought the furniture.

Carefully, I thought it through. Lights, water, and gas were already on. Would it be difficult to have them transferred to my name? I shivered with fear. Should anyone suspect this was not an ordinary move, I'd be in terrible trouble. A telephone could wait if Southern Bell only made hook-ups during the week. Getting in was the important thing.

Ready to make my calls, trembling, I determined to say as little as possible—just the facts. Everything hinged on engaging the same movers who had removed my furniture in January.

I dialed.

"This is Mrs. Stewart. You moved my things from 6395 Vernon Woods Drive after a fire. I'm ready to move back. Will you pick up my furniture this Saturday and deliver it, please?"

Anxiously I prayed while he checked his schedule.

Please, God.

"Yes, ma'am, we can do it. Now what's the address again?"

I completed instructions and quickly called the utility companies. Trying to sound businesslike, I ordered change of service from the apartment to the house, effective the end of the week.

The waiting began. Every day I feared my plan would be exposed. Each time a personal call came for me at work, I suffered a nervous physical reaction. I didn't dare tell any one my plan, sure that they'd try to stop me. Even mother might think it too risky. Common sense arguments might weaken my resolve. I'd call mother on Friday evening. She might be annoyed at being notified so late, but she'd baby-sit anyway. Later I'd explain my secrecy.

Saturday morning I awakened early. Nervously, I checked for clouds. Good! The sun shone brightly. Excitement, mingled with fear, gripped me. I could hardly drink a cup of coffee.

Mother, dependable as always, arrived. She radiated good humor and enthusiasm. How different we were! Even in looks. Taller than me, inclined to a rounder figure, dark hair and shining eyes, plus an infectious smile. She sat and stood erect. Good carriage and courage. I remembered as a child hearing her say, "When I die, put a brick under my chin." The mental image horrified me. Strangers had thought John was her son, me a daughter-in-law. Smaller, fairer, usually serious, I curled my body catlike when sitting. Mother leaned toward life. I retreated.

"You certainly have a beautiful day for going home!" mom said.

"Yes, I'm glad it's not raining. Let's get busy and load your car. Then you'll be ready to come out when I call."

"No. I can do that after you leave. You go on. You have

to watch the movers and stay behind them. Get everything in the proper place. Let them do the heavy work."

Perhaps she sensed my eagerness to hurry. I paused, tempted to tell her how scared I was. What if I couldn't pull it off? What would I do? I'd burned my bridges already, having given up the apartment. Maybe it was crazy to take such a risk. What if I were stopped? Mother interrupted my thoughts.

"Now don't dawdle. We've a lot of work to do today. Call just as soon as you want me to bring the children."

"I'm taking Sue with me." If anything happened, Sue could call a neighbor. She was seven and could carry out instructions. She'd be a help.

As we started out the door, I picked up a tall three-legged stool.

"Mama, why did you bring that? It doesn't belong to us, does it?" Sue asked as we got in the car.

"No. I'm just borrowing it. Our landlady won't mind. It may turn out to be the key to our house."

"What do you mean, mama?"

I looked at the beautiful girl with blonde curly hair and deep blue eyes, like her daddy's. Why did everyone remind me of *him* this morning? Shuddering, I fought nostalgia and tried to relieve Sue's anxious look.

"The doors and windows are all locked, Sister. Remember we couldn't get in last Sunday? I don't want to break any of the glass if I can help it. The workmen may have left the storage room doors open." Explaining to her, I voiced my plans. "You know there is no ceiling in the storage room. The top is open to the roof. If I can climb up, I can get to the top of the carport. That's lower than the main house. Then I can walk on the rafters, or beams or whatever they are, until I get to the flooring where we always intended adding a bathroom and closet. I may have to crawl to there. Then I will have room enough to stand."

"But, mama, how will you get in the upstairs room?"

"Through the door, silly."

"Won't it be locked?"

"No. They wouldn't think to lock inside doors in an attic room," I said firmly, hoping I was right.

Oh, Lord, let them be open. At least one. The one on the carport side of the house, please.

"But if they *are* locked, mama?" Sue persisted.

"Then I'll climb back down and smash a window."

Oh, God, don't let me have to do that. I'd probably cut myself and bleed to death right on the spot.

And, anyway, that's really breaking in, I thought.

In a few minutes we were there. I sucked in my breath. "This is it, honey. We're coming home!"

All right, Lord, it's up to You now. Open those doors.

Everything appeared to be as it was last Sunday. I wondered if the workmen had done anything that week. Checking, I found the doors and windows secured tightly. Slowly I walked toward the storage room and turned the doorknob. It opened! Relief flooded me as I stepped in.

"Quick, Sister, bring the stool from the car. It's light enough for you to carry."

I looked up, trembling.

Oh, Lord, this is going to be worse than I thought. You know I can't even stand to climb the high board at the pool. Heights make me dizzy.

"Here, mama."

I placed the stool against the inside wall and stood on it. "It doesn't make me quite as tall as I'd hoped. Maybe I can brace myself on the diagonal two-by-fours."

"I'll go across the street and borrow a ladder, mama." Sue was anxious to help.

"No, darling, this is our secret. No one will ever know how we got in but you and me." I paused. "Of course, if I fall and break my neck, you'd better go tell Mrs. Burk."

I stood on my tiptoes and reached for the top. Oh, why hadn't I thought to wear gloves? I pulled with all my strength.

Lord, this is ridiculous. I can't even do a chin-up.

"Keep trying," the inner voice urged.

I huffed and puffed, straining with all my might. Finally I felt my body lifting. My hands and face were burning as I gave a mighty heave. "Ohhhhhh" I moaned in pain, now hanging by my arms and elbows across the top.

"Are you all right, mama?"

"Yes. I'm going to make it," I panted, "but my slacks caught on a nail. Try and pull the material away so I can swing my leg up."

"Oh, mama, you're bleeding." Sue was almost crying.

"Not really. It's just a scratch. Never mind. Just pull!"

Tugging hard, she freed the cloth from the nail.

"Good girl!" I praised.

Come on, God, lift!

I pulled the hurt leg up, feeling the sting, and stretched

one arm further over to a beam. My hands were killing me and I'd scraped my torso going over the top, but I'd made it!

Looking down, I held on to the roof beams, panting. "Now, Sue, it's okay. Next I'm going to edge over to the door, go downstairs, and let you in the kitchen. You meet me at the back door. "

My blood pounded! I felt faint. Everything in me seemed to be throbbing. The attic heat was intense. I'd climbed into a furnace!

Perspiring, aching, and desperate, I edged toward the door to the upstairs room.

Oh, God, let the door be open. I'd never make it down again!

It opened easily. In seconds I'd run down the steps and flung open the back door. Hugging my baby, I shouted, "We're home, Sue, really home!"

Dashing through the house and opening windows, I said, "Let the fresh air in. Isn't it wonderful, darling?" Then I remembered the stool and stopped. "Oh, I must unload the trunk and put the stool in the car so we won't forget it. Come help me, Sue." Did she know I was hiding the evidence?

By the time we'd finished, opened the house fully, and unloaded the car, the movers arrived. Perfect timing. I greeted them happily. The two men worked fast and followed my instructions.

In an hour, with everything placed, the driver presented me with a bill.

"Oh, no," I protested, "this is to go to Mr. Paul Pratt, the lawyer."

"Ma'am, I'm supposed to collect from you."

"No. There's a misunderstanding. Your company

knows Mr. Pratt has the authority to pay this. He paid the bill when we moved out, too."

"I don't know nothing about that, ma'am."

"Well, come with me across the street. We'll call your boss from my neighbor's house and he can tell you."

Bettye saw me coming from her kitchen window and had the door open. Her warm embrace helped ease the fear and panic creeping on me again.

"Hello, Suzanne. Glad you're back. What can I do to help?"

"We just need to use your phone, Bettye."

"Come on in."

The driver called his superviser and tried to explain. "He wants to talk to you, ma'am."

I went over the facts with the man on the phone. He put up quite an argument. Impatiently I said, "Well, just look at your own file. You can see Mr. Pratt paid you before. I don't pay these bills. He does. You'll have to collect it from him."

Reluctantly he agreed, "All right, Mrs. Stewart. Just sign the ticket and we'll bill him."

"No!" I roared stubbornly. "I didn't sign anything for you to take my furniture out, and I'm not signing anything for your moving it in. You just tell your driver to come on back!" I gave the telephone to the driver. He uttered a few one-syllable sounds and hung up, shaking his head.

"Okay, ma'am," he said resignedly.

"Thanks, Bettye," I said as we left, wondering what she thought of all this.

We crossed the street, and I paused to watch the truck pull away. Jubilantly, I called to Sue, "Honey, go call Mama Sue on Mrs. Burk's phone. Tell her to come quickly and bring Sydney and Hunt." I walked into the house alone.

*Thank You, God, thank You. This battle's won.
I'll never let them frighten me again. Not phone
calls, letters, or threats. I possess this land. It is mine.
Thank You.*

It was a good prayer. Until the next December I
thought of it many times. Mr. Pratt reacted badly. He
refused to pay the moving company and did bring all
manner of pressure upon me. Someone from his office
called me weekly, either his secretary or his son. Coolly I
reminded them of Mr. Pratt's promise to pay the moving
expenses both ways. Finally, I told them to pay or I'd call
my lawyer and sue Mr. Pratt for harassing me. Instead,
I was sued! Righteous indignation made me determined
to see it through to the end, even going to court if need
be.

In December I received a letter from Jack Etheridge.
It said in part:

> I have persuaded them of the uselessness in suing you.
> They agreed to withdraw the complaint, and I have paid
> the minor court cost fee as a Christmas present from
> Ursula and me. I suppose you know we admire you
> tremendously.

16

Accepted and Understood

"WHEN SUZANNE FIRST met Chuck, she thought it was the Second Coming of Christ," a mutual friend said years later.

On a late summer afternoon in 1961 I entered the historic downtown church which housed the Presbyterian Vocational Guidance Center and headed for the water fountain. Gratefully I swallowed the cold water and closed my eyes in relief from the intense heat outside. Tired from working all day at the welfare department and fearful of rejection, I dreaded the coming encounter.

Suddenly, looking up through the haze in the dark church hallway, I saw vivid, shining eyes through the gloom. Startled, I retreated a step with a gasp. I felt dizzy. All I could see were those eyes!

"Mrs. Stewart?"

Had someone really spoken?

"I'm Chuck Bovee. Forgive me for startling you. I came down to show you the way to our offices. Everyone has gone for the day."

Completely unnerved, I muttered something conventional as my eyes adjusted to the surroundings. Finally I saw the whole man. Average build, dark hair and olive skin, about thirty. We walked up the stairs together.

His small office could barely contain the desk, table, file cabinets, books, and boxes. It was crowded and almost as hot as the street, though an electric fan standing on the table gave some relief.

Mr. Bovee offered me one of the two chairs and courteously began explaining the testing I'd undergo. Still uneasy, I answered as best I could while wondering how I looked. There hadn't been time to check my appearance in a mirror after arriving.

"Is the fan bothering you?" he asked politely.

"Oh, no," I lied, aware of my compulsive gesture to hold my hair every time the fan rotated.

He continued informing me of the center's purpose, then interrupted himself.

"The fan does bother you. Here, change chairs with me." He rose.

"Oh, no, really it doesn't," I insisted, terribly embarrassed and self-conscious. I hardly ever perspired. Now my forehead was damp.

"Well, it bothers me to see your hair blow. Please change." His gentle voice insisted.

How kind he is, I thought as we switched chairs. He's perceptive and smart, too.

An hour later, the first session completed, we left the church together. I'd relaxed somewhat during our talk, appreciating things he'd volunteered about his wife and twins. The test I'd taken proved to be fun.

Tension began building again as Mr. Bovee walked beside me. He was a man who made me feel very feminine. Though I didn't know it then, my fears and nervousness were based on distrust. The disillusioning experience with my husband had severely damaged my confidence in men. Dr. Gutzke said I had lost my reference point when John abandoned us, and that it was enough to cause a nervous breakdown. I survived, he said, because I'd shifted my reference point to Jesus Christ.

"My car is parked in here," Mr. Bovee said at the alley, indicating the back of the church.

Oh, God, please don't let him offer me a ride. I like him, but if he does that I'll never have faith in him.

"Remember your next battery of tests one week from today—same time. It's good to have met you," he smiled.

"Thank you. See you next week!" I smiled back. This was the only perfectly relaxed moment I'd spent with him.

Relieved of some nameless burden, I walked toward the bus stop, not minding the heat or the long walk. I'd met a man who behaved just as I felt a Christian should.

Several meetings later, Chuck proceeded to explain his findings. I faced him expectantly now as a friend and a professional in whom I had absolute confidence.

"You came to the guidance center primarily because at the present time you must work to support yourself and your family," he reviewed.

I nodded. He made things so simple and concrete. If someone had asked me how I happened to be there, I'd have given a life history in reply.

"You trained in dramatics and presently are employed in a job which no longer satisfies, though you want to be in some kind of humanitarian work."

Again I agreed, and he continued.

"You're seeking to discover where you can contribute

the most and be happy. You particularly want a church-related position."

I sat very still.

"It seems to me you are asking two questions to help you come to some decision regarding future employment. One, what abilities and aptitudes do I have? Two, am I suited for Christian work? If so, what?"

He won't think I am, I thought, and stiffened.

"The general intelligence test places you in the top 15 percent of people in your age group. Your high school and college achievements tend to confirm this estimate."

He's saying I'm a "B" person, I thought. I was right about that.

"You took two interest tests," he continued, "and they confirm one another. The Kudor shows you have a high interest in outdoors—91 percent."

"Outdoors? Oh, no. I don't even like to pick up a tennis ball!" I exclaimed.

"It has nothing to do with athletics. It refers more to variety—change—spontaneity. Your second highest interest is musical—85 percent. Again, that doesn't mean you have to be a musician, but you have an appreciation. The third is literary—83 percent. Your lowest scores were computation and clerical."

He must think I'm awfully dumb, I thought.

"The Occupational Inventory shows you highest in artistic and personal-social, and low in science and business. In addition, you appear to like situations where you can express yourself verbally. You like to deal with ideas and to direct more than you like to be directed."

Is he saying I'm bossy? I felt guilt creeping up on me. No, I'm artistic!

"There seems to be a consistent picture throughout the tests and interviews. I received the impression that you're most happy where you can create ideas and stimulate a variety of programs. You'd prefer to help set up a program and let someone else do it."

Does that mean I'm lazy? I listened intently but wouldn't ask the questions that plagued me.

"I believe your strong interest will assist you in some phase of Christian education."

"Oh!" I exclaimed. He thinks I'm good enough! What a relief!

"The trend today is for individuals interested in Christian education to get formal training in this field. However, the present demands for Christian Education Directors and lay workers in the church outweigh the supply. The basic requirements would be a Christian commitment and an interest and willingness to work together on a church team to develop a Christian Education program."

"You really think a church might hire me?" I asked increduously, thinking of my divorce.

"Why not? There is no question of your Christian commitment," he stated.

What happy words to hear! I met with his approval!

Lord, I feel accepted and understood for the first time in my life. Thank You! I feel like I've made it into the most exclusive country club in the world.

"The variety of this type of work would seem to fit your interest and ability patterns. However, your enthusiasm is such that you'd have to tread softly and win hearts before suggesting some of the creative ideas which might come immediately to your mind."

He sees my weaknesses but thinks I'm creative!

"Is that a warning?" I asked playfully, pleased and flattered by his previous statements.

"Probably you tend to vacillate between an abundance of enthusiasm and discouragement. We all do this to some degree."

Now he's going to let me down easy, I thought, discouraged.

"I believe the morass of tradition that quite often surrounds our church programs might get you down."

He doesn't believe in me, I thought, very disappointed.

"But you have something to contribute," he said firmly.

My spirit rose but I felt like crying.

"Your contribution will be directly related to your ability to gracefully cooperate with those you're working with. Push their programs and be concerned about their interest that you might win their confidence and have them open to your ideas."

Well, that's it, I thought. That's all there is. I've got problems to overcome.

"In summary, you have good basic ability. What you lack in skills can be obtained on the job. You'd not be good in a situation where you had to do routine work, such as computational, clerical, or business work."

"So the question now is: Where do I go from here?"

"Suzanne, God has a plan for you. He desires to use you. At the same time, the work will prove satisfactory to you."

He's sincere! He must be right. God will use me. I do have strengths. Some of my scores are high—very high. My life will count for something.

"Thank you, Chuck. All this has been very helpful. I feel better about things."

"I'm interested in your progress. The Lord will open the appropriate door at the right time. Let me know what happens."

He really cares about me.

"I will," I assured him, feeling more than I could express.

Mixed emotions gripped me. Greater expectation for the future mingled with sadness that the interviews were over.

There was no reason to be sad.

17

Supplied

"You're cleaning your desk out like there's no tomorrow," Mrs. Powell said.

"I want to leave things in good shape," I answered.

At 5:00 I left the welfare department with no farewell scenes. Only Mrs. Powell, my latest supervisor, knew I might not return. For months I'd accumulated annual leave. I'd also made applications for a church position. Mrs. Powell agreed to my leave serving as notice time if I made a change while on vacation. She wished me well.

Riding home on the bus I thought wistfully of the security of wives in my neighborhood. Perhaps many were spoiled by having too much. I'd heard several complain:

"I didn't sit down all day. Children have to be watched every minute."

"All I do is pick up and clean behind my maid."

"I spent the entire day chauffeuring children!"

These women who made up some of the garden and bridge clubs bored me, and yet I envied them! They were spared the responsibilities I faced. I'd gladly change my frightening, uncertain future for full-time suburban living. I could learn to like the people and the activities now that I'd experienced a more difficult life.

Jenny's summer with us ended today. This would be the last time she'd meet the bus.

I could see the parked car long before the bus stopped. Jenny held onto Hunt, who leaned far out a window. Spotting me, he waved his arms wildly, calling, "Mama, mama!" The girls popped their pretty heads out the other windows and waved madly. You'd have thought I'd been gone a month.

Thank You, Father, for giving me these loving children. They're not afraid of anything. Help me to be a more trusting child to You, as they are to me.

The next day I began the serious business of adjusting. Schools opened. I drove Sue and Sydney myself, wishing I could do it permanently. The second afternoon as we were coming home, a grating noise alarmed me. Something was dragging under the frame. The car rolled to a stop.

"Mama, what happened?" Sue exclaimed. "Did the motor fall out?"

"I think so, Sister." Actually it was the battery.

We hitchhiked home, and I pondered the problem. The car just wasn't worth spending money on. How could I get rid of it? It couldn't remain on the fashionable street right by the governor-elect's home! I called a used car dealer.

"Don't worry about it, Mrs. Stewart. We'll tow it in and give you $100 credit on another car, sight unseen."

What a relief! I couldn't help but smile, even though worried.

Oh, Lord, my life is ridiculous! We're in need of many things: furniture, clothes, money, now a car. I want a new job, a live-in maid, and a carpool for the girls. I feel helpless and inadequate. Others around us apparently have everything they need, and

I don't have an answer to any of my problems. If You
have a solution, tell me. Send a messenger. I don't
even know which problem to start on. And if You
know anyone who has something I need that he
doesn't care about, get it to me somehow. I will ap-
preciate anything!

Hunt's school furnished transportation. While seeing
him off one morning, I called out, "Give my love to
Mrs. Williams."

The driver, Mrs. Partain, stopped.

"Mrs. Williams isn't with us anymore."

"Oh! Well, who is Hunt's teacher this year?" I asked.

"I'm not sure. We're still a little disorganized. Probably it will be Mrs. Mount, or someone new," she answered.

My mind raced.

"Do you mean you're short a teacher?" I asked.

"Why, yes."

Mrs. Partain seemed surprised I'd asked.

"Not anymore!" I laughed. "You tell the principal not
to hire anyone. I want the job!"

"Are you serious?"

"You better believe it. Tell Mrs. Vernoy I'm coming
over to talk to her as soon as I dress."

"Okay!" Mrs. Partain called after me.

I'd already started running toward the house. I'd borrow Bettye's car to drive to Fritz Orr.

A few days later, Jean Mount, a pretty, soft-spoken
woman, chatted with me on Fritz Orr's spacious playground. She taught Hunt, as Mrs. Vernoy thought it
best he not be in my group. Our two classes were playing together.

"Oh, Jean, I'm so happy. It is glorious to be outside
where I can watch my son climbing, running, and play-

ing. This is heaven compared to working downtown in those dreary, noisy buildings."

"Yes, it is nice here, especially for the little ones," she agreed.

"I can't get over how miraculously this job meets my needs. I don't mind driving the bus at all since they let me keep it at home and use it for personal errands. It saves me from buying a car. I can take my daughters to Lovett School since it's so close, and I don't have to have a maid. It's just perfect!"

"Except for the salary," Jean said.

"True. True. That's the only fly in the ointment. I really don't know how I can make do with it, but I will. There are all the nice things to think about: free tuition for Hunt, a wonderful place to give children's birthday parties, and being close to Mrs. Vernoy. I'll learn a lot from her. She's wonderful."

"Yes," Jean replied, "Sadie Vernoy is the most remarkable woman I've ever known. She loves everybody."

"And the air!" I inhaled. "I just love breathing here. What an atmosphere." Standing near the pony ring, I could see the playing field, tennis courts, swimming pool, and stables. "What a glorious place!"

Jean nodded.

"Why in the world did Mrs. Williams give up such a lovely job?" I asked.

"I don't know. She didn't talk much, but I guess she was unhappy. Last year she and her husband were divorced. Her little boy was in my class then. I know it bothered her—the divorce, I mean. I thought things were working out. She didn't have any financial problems. Her mother is wealthy, and her husband's a responsible man. I don't know what happened. She seemed well adjusted and looked marvelous when school started."

"You mean last week?" I asked, much surprised.

"Yes. She started the year with us. We were all together at a teachers' meeting. She was apparently fine, friendlier than usual really. I remember the way she put on her little white gloves and said good-by, she'd see us tomorrow."

"And she didn't come the next day?" I prodded.

"No. We never saw her again. She checked into a downtown hotel after she left us that day."

Suddenly it seemed very quiet on the playground. I tried to hear the children. A bird sang. Surely Jean wouldn't say what I was thinking. Surely not.

Jean sighed with a shudder.

"She killed herself."

18

A Different Christmas

"Everything's ready. Supper's cooked. The guest room is made up for Ceal and Willa," I told mother on the phone. "I'm just waiting for you."

"We're leaving the station right now. I just wanted to check," mother answered and hung up.

I'd told the truth. Everything had been done. Tomorrow was Christmas Eve. School holidays had given me time to prepare for mother's dear friend Ceal and her daughter, Willa, who were coming from Florida. Mother had suggested I let them stay at my house. I agreed, feeling the Lord had provided me with the house and anyone He sent should be welcome.

Perfectly relaxed, I added tinsel to the enormous Christmas tree in the living room. It had been in my carport one day when I drove in from Fritz Orr. The first surprise of the season! Joyce had brought it to me as a gift from Kent who was selling trees as a Kiwanis project.

My friends continued to help me generously. Joyce, Lettie, and Rosemary gave me clothes their children had outgrown. Doris and Frank Boggs made sure I enjoyed a little social life. They gave beautiful parties and included me on the guest list. Doris often asked me to serve, making sure I'd have opportunity to meet and chat with everyone. Frank, a professional singer, had a host of friends near and far. Any out-of-town guests provided an excellent reason to entertain.

The ham in the oven, smelling delicious, and turkey in the refrigerator came from Doris. She said they'd been given two of each from friends and had no room to store the extras.

All these friends had presents under the tree for my children. And I had more gifts than ever in my life! The children in my class and those who rode with me had all given me presents. I'd saved them to open Christmas morning. For as long as I could remember, I'd wanted lots and lots of different surprises. Usually I'd had one or two big items and a few lesser things. I looked forward gleefully to opening each gaily wrapped box.

My toys for the children were hidden in the trunk of mother's car. Sue, Sydney, and Hunt had explored every drawer, closet, and even the attic rafters. Several times I had discovered one of them peeking under a bed or behind draperies.

The telephone rang, interrupting my thoughts.

"Suzanne?"

Mother's voice was recognizable but very strange.

"Some drunk hit my car from behind and we're all in Grady Hospital."

"Mother! Are you hurt?"

"I don't know how bad off we are. I'm cut up and something's broken. Ceal's leg is broken, but I think Willa is all right."

"Mom, I'll be right there."

Anticipated Christmas scenes disappeared. Hospitals, antiseptic, uniforms and odors, pain, and horror came to mind. No tinsel gaiety now. Stark reality. My hands shook and I trembled as I hung up the phone. What must I do? Quickly I dialed Lettie.

"Lettie, mom's been in a wreck. May I bring the children by your house so I can get to her?"

"Of course!" Lettie replied immediately. "Is she hurt badly?"

"I don't know. I'll call you from the hospital."

I gripped the steering wheel and tried not to speed. Mother had often said, "It is best to assume everyone on the road is crazy, drunk, and out to get you!"

She would never weave in or out of lanes, or even be on the expressway, as I was now. How ironic she should be in an accident. Traffic slowed as I came closer to the downtown area. Soon I was bumper to bumper with last-minute shoppers and party-goers.

Oh, Lord, I could scream. Please get me through.

Arriving at the hospital, I saw sixteen-year-old Willa immediately. She'd been waiting at the door for me. Thank God she wasn't hurt! She burst into tears when I put my arms around her.

"Oh, it was awful. We were stopped at a red light when he hit us from the back. His car went to the left and crashed into one on the other side. Your mother hit the man in front of her, and he went into a parked car on the right. There were five cars in all. I was thrown out."

"Where's your mother, Willa? Where's mine?"

Moments later I found my mother lying on a stretcher, unattended, in a large, dimly lit room upstairs.

"Mom!" How could the hospital just leave her like this?

"Suzanne, that drunk didn't even have a license! We had to ride in the same ambulance. They laid him down and made me sit up! My bones were broken and he was just dead drunk. His liquor odor made me ill. I almost threw up!"

Her voice became almost a whimper at times—so unlike the anger and indignation she felt.

"Mother, have you had anything for pain?"

"No," her voice rose a little, "they haven't done anything for me, except let me call you. And I think I paid the ambulance bill for that drunk, too!"

"Mom, I've got to get you out of here—I've got to get you moved to a private hospital. The emergency room here will be filled all night because everyone is brought to Grady first. Now please be brave a little longer and let me go make arrangements."

"Ceal, too. I want Ceal with me."

"Yes, of course. I'll be right back."

I went to the phone and called Dr. Broyles. He'd gone to a Christmas party. I dialed our associate minister. He was at a Christmas party, too. Then I tried Jack Etheridge.

Dear God, help me. Is everybody out celebrating? I don't know how to get mom and Ceal out of this hospital into another. Someone must tell me.

"Jack's not here. He and Ursula have gone to a Christmas party. My wife and I are baby-sitting," Jack's stepfather told me.

Some party, I thought, irritated at not having been invited. Obviously it was given by someone in the church.

"May I ask why you're calling?" he prodded.

"Oh, yes! My mother's been hurt in an automobile wreck. I've got to get her moved from Grady to Piedmont Hospital and I don't know how. I called Dr. Broyles and Mr. Freeman and now Jack. Everybody seems to be at that party."

"My dear," he spoke crisply, "you don't need a minister or a lawyer. You need a doctor!"

"Oh, of course! Why didn't I think of that? Thank you."

Dr. Robert Wells came immediately to mind.

Dear God, please let him be home.

What a relief to hear his voice answering! I gave him the information and he promptly reassured me.

"I'll call and order a sedative for your mother at once, Suzanne. Don't worry. You take the young girl somewhere for the night. I'll call an ambulance for your mother and her friend and you can meet us at Piedmont in the emergency room."

Then I dialed Lettie to tell her I was bringing Willa.

"Of course. We've got plenty of food and beds. She'll be fine here. How's your mother?"

"I don't know. She has lots of cuts, a broken arm, and something's the matter with her neck."

"Maybe a broken collarbone?"

"I suppose so. Her friend's leg is broken."

"Those injuries will all mend in time. Thank God they weren't hurt worse."

"Yes, but, Lettie, this is awful. Seeing mother lie there helpless. You know how active and independent she is."

"Yes. I wish I could be with you. I've called Rosemary and Joyce—Doris, too—but they're all at Christmas parties."

"So were the people I called first—all but you."

"Guess you and I were the only ones at home alone, as usual," she laughed. "Rex is out every night."

I hurried back to mother, longing to give her some peace of mind. She'd never had to rely on me before. Would she have confidence in the decisions I made?

By her side, I explained the plans, trying not to sound uneasy myself. Her docility frightened me.

"Who is Dr. Wells?" she asked.

"He's a wonderful orthopedic specialist. You'll like him. And he's tall, dark, and handsome."

I tried to comfort and amuse her until a nurse brought medication. Then I kissed her and left.

Willa, usually quiet, was even quieter as we drove to Lettie's.

"Everything will be all right, Willa. No one was hurt critically. I don't know why God permitted this to happen, but we can thank Him anyway. He'll use it for good in our lives. Believe that. Tonight you're going to stay with a friend of mine. She's a fine Christian woman and will take good care of you. My children are there now. Tomorrow I'll take you to my house, and we'll visit the hospital, of course. It will be a different Christmas, but we can still have a happy one."

Already I thought of decorating the hospital room. I'd get two little trees for the tables, mistletoe to pin on their pillows, and holly from my own bushes. Suddenly it seemed very important for Mother, Ceal, and Willa to have as much of Christmas as possible. I could open my gifts later tonight, alone, and make a list of them for thank-you notes. That would be fun! Then I'd select what would be given to Mom, Ceal, and Willa and rewrap them so they'd have lots of things to open. Most of the gifts surely would be things any female could enjoy: cosmetics, jewelry, books. I'd slip Willa's under our tree and take mom's and Ceal's to the hospital room when they were asleep.

I took Willa in to meet Lettie, talked to my children who were watching television, then rushed to Piedmont. I was there when the ambulance arrived. Mom and Ceal were put in an emergency room and then X-rays were taken. While I was waiting with mother for Dr. Wells, the door opened and Joyce entered, looking beautiful in green satin with a white fur piece.

"Why, Joyce," I said, "you were at a party."

"Yes, but now I'm here with you," she said cheerfully.

She stayed, too. Hours passed, during which broken bones were set and Dr. Wells operated on mother. Finally the two friends lay side by side in a semi-private room. In the early morning hours, satisfied we could do nothing else, we left.

"Where now?" Joyce asked.

"Down to police headquarters. Someone told me the toys in mom's trunk flew all over Piedmont Road. The policemen gathered them up and I'm supposed to claim them."

"I'll drive you. We can pick up your car on the way back."

"Thank you, Joyce. I won't argue. You'd go anyway, and I'm glad to have your company!"

We were both astonished at the activity in the police station at such an hour. It was as active as a downtown department store at noon. We were shown to the salvage room where I recognized our things. A shopping bag of extra linens mother was bringing showed blood stains throughout. Most of the toys were ruined. A little truck for Hunt was badly dented.

"I'll give this to him anyway. I'll write a note from Santa saying that since grandmother had a wreck, he thought Hunt would like a truck that had had one too."

"Kent bought too many things for our boys. I'll bring some over tomorrow."

Tears filled my eyes. What would I do without friends?

Dawn was breaking when Joyce left me at my car. By the time I got home, the sun was rising. Strange, entering an empty house on Christmas Eve day, but I just had to sleep a couple of hours before getting the children.

A special delivery letter had been stuck in the door. Unemotionally, I opened it, recognizing John's writing. A slip of paper fluttered to the floor as I pulled out a money order for $25.00. I picked up the fallen note and read with tired, dull eyes:

> Suzanne,
>   This is all I have. Please get a little present for each of the children from me for Xmas to put under the tree. I *am* going to make a *lot* of money in 1962. We *have* gone through the worst of it. Like Scarlett says "we are never going to be poor again" (I hope).
>   Merry, merry Christmas,
>
> John

We? When did *we* ever go through anything together? It's *me*. I'm the one going through it.

Exhausted as never before in my life, one thing more must be done before I slept.

I wrote John in care of his mother.

> Dear John,
>   From now on, if you want the children to have a present from you, you'll have to send it yourself.
>
> Best wishes,
> Suzanne

19

Everybody Has One

"You DON'T HAVE any money do you?" Arron asked, teasing my hair vigorously.

"Not much. Maybe a dollar or two," I answered.

"I mean: *you really don't have any money?*" he emphasized each word.

"Not accumulated, invested, or stashed away. What are you getting at?"

"I knew she was lying," Arron stated flatly, characteristically cocking his head of groomed, glistening black hair to one side.

"Who?"

No answer. Accustomed to his sudden lapses into silence, I didn't attempt conversation. Nor did I try to figure out the temperamental hairdresser. Instead, I thought about my financial condition since he'd brought up the subject.

Things had been difficult. The salary I earned with the Fritz Orr School hardly covered my utilities, especially now in winter when the heat bill ran high. I'd taken every odd job offered me. One afternoon a week I taught a modeling class in a charm school. The young couple across the street left their three little girls with me when they went out of town on frequent weekend trips. His company often paid expenses for them to attend meetings and conventions. Once they went away for a whole week! Mrs. Vernoy let me bring the girls to Fritz Orr every day, so I made a lot of money then. Somehow we were getting by, but obviously there was no future for me in nursery school teaching. I'd finish the year, but then it would be necessary to get a better paying job.

Oh, Father, I hate to think of it. I love being with Hunt, and he needs me. My daughters do, too. Why must things be like this? I enjoy this work. If only I had some regular income to supplement, it would be ideal. Please work things out so I can stay close to home one more year.

"I told Julia it couldn't be true," Arron spoke.

"What?"

I'd forgotten what he was talking about.

"Remember Julia's son had an automobile wreck a couple of weeks ago? She said you came over to her house one day while she was at the hospital."

"So?" I said, trying not to show my discomfort. Julia lived in Sandy Springs and worked for Arron occasionally. I hadn't thought of her telling. Good works should be done in secret.

"Julia found a pot of homemade vegetable soup on the stove, a note from you, and money on the counter. She thought you'd left it. I told her she was crazy: you didn't have any money."

"That's for sure!" I agreed.

Wishing I could get his mind on something else, my eyes scanned the room from left and right. I could see through the doorway into Arron's reception area. Three pictures of me hung over the mantlepiece. They were from a newspaper article, and Arron said each was worth $1,000 to him. I remembered how the article had come about. One Saturday morning I'd left his salon absolutely amazed at his artistry. He had created a most unusual and becoming hairstyle for me. At home, I impulsively called a friend who was women's editor of the local paper.

"Edith, I haven't time to talk, and you probably don't either. Take my word for this: You ought to do a story on my hairdresser. He has made a raving beauty of me. I look adorable. He's outdone himself today—really genius at work. I'm on my way downtown to a fashion show. I know hardly any of the staff are at the newspaper office on Saturday, but if a photographer is on duty, I'll stop by and have pictures made. I know you'll want to do a feature on Arron when you see this hairstyle, if it photographs well. Will you call and arrange for photos? Call me back quickly and let me know. Okay?"

She took my word, made the calls, and seemed delighted with the results. The next week we worked on the story together by phone. I marveled at Edith's ability to handle an interview, type, and listen at the same time! The result was a highly amusing article with several pictures covering six columns.

The publicity thrilled Arron in a way no tangible gift ever could. He claimed it had doubled his business.

Thank You, Lord, for bringing this to pass. All I did was appreciate his talent and act as a channel. Make me a channel of blessing for many.

"Well, did you do it?" he asked. His long slender fingers pressed my hair on each side and his dark eyes challenged my reflection in the mirror.

"Arron, you know good and well I have more ideas than money," I teased.

"The money was the fishy thing. I believed you took

the soup. Your mother made it, didn't she?" His face relaxed into a knowing smile.

"Yes."

"I knew it. I've had her soup before. It's good. But the money—who left that?"

Lord, should I tell him or keep quiet?

I was in a quandary. How could Arron understand giving money away when it was badly needed? Ideas, yes. Soup, yes. Money, no! I felt a little guilty facing the thought of his giving me complete hair care for nothing. He provided permanents and color when needed, as well as cuts, shampoos, and sets. I believed a Christian should give, sacrificially if necessary, where there is a need. Julia needed supportive friendship but not money, as I knew now. The soup and note would have shown her I cared. Perhaps I'd overdone it. I'd always needed cash badly, so it was easy to think everyone did—in any misfortune.

Julia had come to my house shortly after my visit to hers.

"Suzanne, I can't tell you how much it meant for you to do what you did."

"Oh, Julia, it wasn't much. I am so sorry about the accident."

"Thank you. We came home tired and hungry. The soup tasted marvelous. Just what we needed. And your sweet note touched me deeply. I wouldn't take anything in the world for what you did, but I want you to take the money back."

She laid the bills on the table in front of the sofa.

"I appreciate this and would keep it if we needed it, but honestly, we don't. The insurance company will pay for just about everything."

"I didn't know."

"We were lucky that it happened at a time when we're doing pretty well and have a little money. I assure you, we've seen days when this would have been a blow financially as well as emotionally. You keep this money to help the next person."

The next person is me, I thought, glad to have it back.

Now, what could I tell Arron? He spoke again.

"I told Julia you couldn't have left the money. You're poor!"

I just sat there. Mute.

"You are poor, aren't you?"

"I'm very poor. I'm probably the only person in Sandy Springs, maybe Atlanta, who's so poor that I don't have a refrigerator!"

I'd spoken seriously, then got tickled watching his reaction in the mirror. He stopped combing and stared with dumbfounded amazement, changing slowly to disbelief. I grinned.

"You're kidding," he said. "Everybody has a refrigerator."

"I don't."

"How in the world can you live without one?" he exclaimed.

"It poses some problems. I tried keeping the milk, eggs, and butter in the outside milkbox. The carport's cold enough to keep things from spoiling, but the neighborhood dogs took the butter and ate it. Then I made sort of a make-do icebox by putting things in a roaster on a high stool. The dogs knocked the whole thing over and ran away with my bacon!"

"Are you kidding me?" Arron asked, suspicious of my smile.

"Good heavens, no!"

He was completely distracted from thinking about the Julia episode, I noticed with satisfaction.

"Why don't you have a refrigerator?"

"Remember I brought mom to my house after she was dismissed from the hospital? She needed someone to help her sit up and get dressed. While she was staying with me, the refrigerator went on the blink. The repairman said they'd have to take it in to fix it. He estimated repairs would be at least eighty dollars, maybe over a hundred. That depressed me! Mother heard our conversation and called me to her room. She waved her good arm dramatically and, like a queen giving a command, said, 'Don't send it out. Call those friends of yours who have the junk shop in Smyrna. Tell them they can have the refrigerator. And your washer and dryer, too, if they'll come and get them. Get rid of all those appliances. They couldn't be any good after going through the fire. When I get out of here, I'll get you new ones. Someone's always moving and selling such things. I can pick them up for a song!' You know mother's in the real estate business, Arron. I thought she'd be able to do it, so I gave them away."

"Did the washer and dryer work?"

"The washer did, but the dryer had been out of commission for awhile."

"And you've been living without a refrigerator ever since?"

"Yes."

"I wonder why you kept the stove?"

I laughed. It did sound crazy. At the time, I had thought it logical.

"Mother meant well. I don't think she had any idea how long she'd be handicapped. Neither did I. She's back at home now but not yet driving, so she can't find these great bargains. She's short of money, too. The wreck was costly.

Her car was totaled. The man who hit her had no in-surance. She has her problems."

"How are you managing now?"

"I keep a few things outside covered by the milkbox upside down with a brick on it. Sometimes the dogs push it around, but they can't lift it!"

"How awful!"

"It's not too bad. I do sort of wonder what we'll do when warm weather comes though."

We were both silent while he finished the comb-out. Then he ordered: "Follow me."

We walked through the salon, out the front door, and down the gravel driveway to a terrace entrance. Entering his apartment, we walked through the living room and kitchen. He stopped and lit a candle, saying nothing, then mysteriously opened a locked door. An unfinished cellar was exposed.

"Come on," he said.

Creeping behind him, I smelled the cold clay, then followed the candle's light with my eyes as he gestured to the left.

"There!" he said triumphantly. "There is your new refrigerator."

I saw an apartment-size appliance. Very small compared to my old one with the huge freezer, but very large compared to a milk container!

"Oh, Arron!" I shouted gleefully, "does it work?"

"Of course."

"And I can have it?"

"For twenty-five dollars. You do have twenty-five dollars, don't you?"

"Yes!" I laughed.

Thanks to Julia!

20

Don't Hang up too Soon

SILENCE FRIGHTENED ME sometimes.

Riding home from Fritz Orr one bright June morning, I felt uneasy. The school year had come to an end, and plans were made for the glorious summer day camp program. College boys and girls assisted the staff in teaching diving, swimming, horseback riding, crafts, and all the other sports and activities imaginable.

"Your children can come free, Suzanne, if you'll drive a group back and forth," Mrs. Vernoy had offered.

I agreed readily. Miraculous! All three of my children enjoying the best summer program available in the most exclusive area of Atlanta. Wealthy men provided such privileges for their children. God provided for mine.

But what would I do? I felt alone.

"Why are you afraid?" asked the inner voice.

Money, I guess. I don't know what to do. The future looks so empty.

"Have I been so long with you, and you still fear?"

I'm sorry. I know better. You've taken care of us wonderfully.

"Then why be afraid?"

It's me. I just don't know what to do, and I feel so helpless.

"What have you done?"

I applied for unemployment insurance.

"And you're eligible?"

Yes, thank You. That gives me a little income for the summer.

"What else have you done?"

I've been in touch with some modeling contacts.

"What more can you do?"

I don't know. Let me think.

I hardly realized that my fear had disappeared and my senses were responding once again to the world around me. The trees and grass were bright green, the sky vivid blue and white. I heard the occasional bark of a dog and my tires squealing as I rounded the curves on Mt. Paran Road. The smell of freshly cut grass floated through the open windows along with a whiff of wild onions. Summer is fun time! Many families would be planning vacations.

Vacations! That's it. I could try to fill in for people going out of town.

The inner voice didn't answer, but I felt approval as I thought of various possibilities. As soon as I arrived home, I worked on the new idea. Sitting on the bed, telephone in hand, I began leafing through the yellow pages of the telephone directory.

I tried radio stations, television stations, and special schools. The first several calls gave no encouragement. Other staff members took on absent employees' duties. My enthusiasm quickly subsided, and I wanted to quit and go swimming. Forcing myself to keep at it, I saw a listing for the Atlanta Speech School. Might as well try. God couldn't help me if I made no effort. I must try, disheartened or not.

"The Atlanta Speech School. Good morning."

"Good morning. My name is Suzanne Stewart. I'm calling because I have some experience in teaching. If any of your teachers are going to be away for vacation, perhaps I could fill in temporarily."

"You're a teacher of the deaf?"

"No. I majored in drama in college and minored in speech. But I've been teaching at Fritz Orr School."

"I don't quite understand. Are you looking for a job?"

"Not exactly. I will be soon, when summer's over. I have to work but can't take a full-time job now because I'm driving a group of children back and forth to Fritz Orr Camp. I'm trying to find something to do during the in-between hours. Do you need any helpers?"

"Our teachers all have to have special training. The Junior League does all the voluntary work. But you sound as though you'd be very good working with our children. Have you ever thought of going back to school and getting certified in speech and hearing?"

"Oh, no! I couldn't possibly do that. I have to work."

"Are you sure you couldn't consider getting further training? We have some scholarships available. Let me connect you with Dr. McCroskey. He's in charge of our student-teacher program. Hold on, please."

"All right." A thrill of anticipation flashed through me. I hardly understood what she had been saying, but she sounded so eager. When a marvelously masculine voice spoke, I reacted as if coming to attention!

"Mrs. Stewart? I'm Dr. McCroskey."

His voice alerted me. It was filled with vitality as well as virility.

"I'm the Director of Speech here. Also, I'm on the staff at Emory University. We're looking for people who qualify to enter our profession. It sounds as if you might have the right background."

"Actually, I had hoped to help on your teaching staff this summer as a replacement or aide."

"What degree do you hold?"

"In drama."

"And what kind of work have you done?"

"After college I did TV and stage work until I married. More recently I've been a welfare worker and a teacher."

"You like working with children?"

"Yes. Adults, too. I scored high in the personal-social area of the vocational guidance tests I took."

"I'd like to see all your test scores. Have you ever considered getting a master's degree?"

"Yes, once. When I was first married we lived in Danville, Virginia, and I considered entering school at the University of North Carolina in Chapel Hill. But I decided it was too far to commute."

"We have an excellent speech and hearing program at Emory University."

"I'm afraid it's too late for me. I can't afford it now." And I doubt if I'm smart enough, I added silently.

"We have several grants available. If something could be worked out about your tuition, perhaps you might find the idea more feasible?"

"I don't know. I've never thought of Emory. This takes me by surprise."

"Tell you what. Let me send you some things to read. You look them over, then come talk to me. I think you should see the Atlanta Speech School. This is the clinical setting in which you will do most of your work as an Emory student."

He said "will," not "would." Are You speaking through him?

"Thank you. That would be nice."

"How about our making an appointment for you to come here Friday morning at ten? That allows time for you to receive the brochure about the Atlanta Speech School in the mail. I'll include an application for a grant and a sheet describing the procedures for being admitted to full standing in the graduate program in the field of speech and hearing pathology. Read them carefully and we'll discuss them Friday."

"All right. Friday at ten."

"I'll go ahead and notify the graduate school office to send you a graduate bulletin and application for admission. You should receive them within a day or two. If not, let me know and I'll see if I can speed them up."

"All right."

"I'm looking forward to meeting you in person, Mrs. Stewart. Glad you called."

"Thank you."

After completing the call, I slipped to my knees by the side of the bed. The conversation so overwhelmed me that I forgot my aversion to praying on the floor. I'd been reluctant to kneel ever since living in the squalid apartment where I'd feared a rat might run across my feet.

Oh, Father. Is this part of Your plan for me? It is incredible! I'm mystified. What an enormous idea. Wouldn't it be wonderful to have a master's? We haven't had one in the family in over two generations. My ancestors were doctors and ministers before the First World War and the Depression. A speech and hearing pathologist! That would really be something to be proud of! How could I do it, though, with no money? It sounds insane.

"Not insane. Improbable."

But it is a good thing, isn't it?

"Yes."

If it's Your will, it could be done, couldn't it?

"Yes."

Well, I wouldn't dare tell a soul I'm even thinking of such a thing. They'd say I was crazy!

"Yes. They said that about Me, too."

21

Vital Encounter

SITTING IN THE lobby of the Atlanta Speech School, I willfully relaxed my hands and arms, trying to look completely at ease. The lobby buzzed with activity. I tried to interest myself in the people there, but kept my eyes shifting to the staircase. After announcing me, the receptionist had said, "Dr. McCroskey will be down in a moment."

I knew him the second he appeared. He smiled a message directly to me. Without appearing to hurry, he moved swiftly down the steps and across the room, speaking warmly to each person he passed. He looked like a man who enjoyed college enough to keep the outer manifestations: a crew cut, glasses, bow tie, and pullover sweater. He definitely was my generation. Those of us who went to high school in the late forties bore the marks. He looked like a football player who had danced to the music of Glenn Miller and Tommy Dorsey.

"Mrs. Stewart?"

I rose to grasp his outstretched hand.

"I'm Bob McCroskey. This is your first visit to the Speech School?"

"Yes."

Resting his hand lightly under my elbow, he guided me across the room.

"Here is the library. Our Emory students study and have classes there. Only a few are taught on the campus. On the right is our diagnostic clinic. One day a week we do testings and evaluations. The other four days our Speech School and the Oral School for the Deaf have regular hours. Let's go up."

As we mounted the stairs, he continued giving me information.

"In addition to our schools and clinic, others come for individual lessons. Mrs. Byrd is working with a boy who has an articulation problem."

We paused at her door at the top of the stairs. Smiles were exchanged, but the lesson was not interrupted.

"Across the hall, Miss Ramsey is teaching aphasic children."

He led me into an alcove where we peered through a one-way mirror at a group of five children and the teacher. Dr. McCroskey turned up the sound, and we listened briefly.

Further down the hall, he paused again before a glass.

"This is our Diagnostic Class. These children have problems that could not be positively identified in our clinic. We let them come for a month, during which time they're observed by specialists in many fields. A speech and hearing therapist, otologist, psychologist, and neurologist. Then a staffing is held and the diagnosis agreed upon. The little girl you see constantly going around and around is probably autistic."

I couldn't say a word. Half his vocabulary was foreign to me.

By the time we arrived at his office, I desperately wanted to be a part of this tremendous work. Would it ever be possible?

When we were comfortably seated, Dr. McCroskey

opened a file folder with my name on it. I'd sent him a copy of the vocational guidance report.

"It looks as if you're good material for our program, Mrs. Stewart. Did you read the literature I sent you?"

"Yes. I am to send a copy of my University of Georgia transcript and two personal references to you?"

"The references to me and the transcript to the graduate school office. They'll need a medical report, too. You're in good health I assume?"

"Yes. My biggest worry is taking the Emory Qualifying Exam tomorrow."

"Nothing to it. You won't have any trouble—with your intelligence."

"I've been out of school a long time."

"Many of our students are older than you. They're often the most highly motivated."

"I am deeply interested in the idea of helping handicapped children."

"Not just children. We have an adult program too. Some of them stutter, lisp, and lose their hearing! Accidents and strokes cause aphasia. A professor of mine used to say 'The speech therapist will get you somewhere between the cradle and the grave.'"

I laughed. "Sounds like a profession where you'd always have a job."

"Right. There's a great need for well-trained people. When you get through our course, you'll be qualified to work in a public school, special education school, clinic, or hospital."

"Getting started sounds incredible. Getting through impossible!"

"Won't three quarters of paid tuition be incentive to start? You can finish in four quarters. That's three-fourths of your total tuition."

"Yes, it's quite generous. If I get that far, I'm sure the fourth quarter tuition money will come from somewhere."

"You may be able to get a government loan. They encourage higher education by allowing you to pay later. If you're employed in the public schools, they reduce the amount each year, up to five years, and then you begin payment of only 50 percent of the original loan."

"Does the money have to go for tuition, or could it be used for living expenses?"

"Either. It is purely a loan."

We talked for another half hour, and I left exhilarated. Before I arrived at mother's, Dr. McCroskey's stimulating personality had faded to the background and doubts assailed me.

"How did the interview go?" mother asked eagerly. I could sense she wanted to know every detail.

"Fine. Dr. McCroskey promised me a nine-hundred dollar scholarship. But, mom, how can I do it? We almost starved to death last year. At least then I had a small income."

"Things have a way of working out," she said happily.

"I can do some part-time work, but I'll have to borrow so much. Emory is such an expensive school and so far away. Dr. McCroskey said some of the classes are taught on campus and some at the Speech School. How can I manage three locations without a car?"

"We'll manage with mine until you get started. You'll meet people who go back and forth." Her eyes twinkled.

"And Sue and Sydney. How can I keep them in private school?"

"I'll pay their tuition this year."

"Mom, I love you for wanting to, but you don't have the money either."

"Things are bound to develop in real estate. I'll go

over and talk to Lovett's treasurer—Mr. Rabbe isn't it? I will assume complete financial responsibility."

Obviously there was no way to get a negative response from mother. She really was pleased at the prospect of my improving myself, and that made me happy.

After talking with mother, I called Chuck Bovee and asked his opinion.

"You'd be well suited to working with people, Suzanne. Though I don't know much about speech and hearing, it sounds compatible with your talents. Apparently it's what we've been praying for."

Next I called Dr. Gutzke. He expressed delight over the news, and I asked him for a reference.

Then I called Dr. Broyles. After the usual greetings, I told him about the possibility before me.

"Do you think I should try for a master's?"

"Why not? I wouldn't have given a nickel for your chances to survive three years ago and you've come this far."

"I've never taken a step of faith like this before. How can four of us live for a year with no income?"

"You didn't have any three years ago."

"That's true. Now I have had the experience of working and getting by. I have the house, too. We didn't have that then."

"It's a miracle you survived."

"And now you think this new venture is possible?"

"No, I don't, but you've never been restricted to the possible. Your faith has carried you places I've never been. Why I've seen you make bricks without straw. It won't surprise me to see you make them without mud."

He, too, promised to send a recommendation to Dr. McCroskey.

Then I drove to the Unemployment Office. After signing, I crossed the street and entered the chapel of Central Presbyterian Church.

Lord, I should feel happy over my good fortune. With mother, Chuck, Dr. Broyles, and Dr. Gutzke all pulling for me, it would seem this is the thing to do. I want to. I'd like to. I'm just not sure I should.

The chapel was quiet and peaceful. Cool, too.

You know how tired I am of struggling. Can I start this thing and endure to the end? No. Not unless I'm absolutely certain this is Your plan for my life. Your will, not mine or Dr. McCroskey's.

"Think back to the beginning."

The beginning for us, the Lord and me, meant the summer of 1959—after John left home in May and before he left the state in January of 1960. I had prayed and read the Bible searching for an answer to our problems. One night the word "disciple" seemed to mean me, too, not just the original twelve. The back of my neck tingled. My heart pounded.

Lord. Lord Jesus, do you want me to be a disciple?

"Yes."

But I'm no good. I have nothing to offer.

"Yourself. I want to join My life to yours. I will take care of you."

Oh, Lord, I've paid You so little attention. I never

*realized before that You are really alive! How can
You forgive me? How can You care?*

"I love you. You are valuable to me."

*Then take my life, please. Use it any way You want.
I've wasted it. If You can use it for anything, I give
it to You gladly.*

"I will live in You. You will be My witness. You will
be a blessing. You will do My work."

That was our vital encounter in 1959. Since then, I'd
often felt His presence and guidance. Now in the summer
of 1962 I prayed:

*Lord, Your will, not mine. I'm just as weak as ever.
No matter what others think. You know without
You I am nothing. I don't have it in me to go to
graduate school. If You want to go through me, that's
the only way.*

I lifted my head and gazed at the beautiful stained-glass
windows in front of me. Slowly I turned and looked at
the one on my right. It was an artist's concept of Jesus
healing the sick. Something inside me seemed to leap
in recognition as I stared.

*The healing ministry! Speech and hearing are part
of Your healing ministry. You opened the ears of
the deaf and made the dumb to speak!*

"Yes. I still do—through My disciples."

22

Not a Hair out of Place

SATURDAY MORNING I left the girls with my neighbor, Bettye, and took Hunt to a friend's house.

"The exam shouldn't take long. I'll be back for him in a couple of hours," I told Jenny Pope.

Three hours later, the person administering the test said, "Please put down your pencils. You've completed the first two sections of the five-part exam. We will break for lunch now. It is noon. Please return to your seats by one o'clock."

I broke the speed limit getting to Jenny's. When she opened the door, I burst into tears.

"Oh, Jenny, I must have been out of my mind. I thought the test would take an hour or so. Dr. McCroskey made it sound like nothing. Why, it lasts *all day*. We're supposed to be back at one. I'm not going. I've got to get home to Sue and Sydney."

Jenny put her arms around my shoulders and led me inside.

"Now, now," she soothed, "of course you're going back."

"No!" I answered vehemently, "I've already flunked it anyway. It's in five parts. We had literature and English this morning. They're my best subjects, and I know I failed. It was so hard! This afternoon is math, science and music-art. I couldn't possibly pass. There's no point in going back. Where's Hunt?"

"He's in the backyard playing with Betsy. We can keep him this afternoon, and Bettye will be glad to keep Sue and Sydney. We'll call her and explain. Let me get you something to eat."

"Oh, I can't. There isn't time to eat," I protested, still sniffling, but Jenny led me to the dining room table. She placed a bowl of soup before me, and I calmed down as the aroma reached my nostrils. She brought a sandwich and tea next, then sat beside me.

Soon I felt refreshed, whether by Jenny's love and manner or her food, I don't know. Nourished, I returned to Emory, grim but determined to try.

As it turned out, I made a higher grade on the General Culture Qualifying Exam than I did on most of the more scientific ones to follow.

After completing that requirement, one thing was left to do. I must send in a medical report. I hated to spend the money, for I'd never needed a doctor except to deliver my babies. Rosemary recommended her neighbor, Dr. Louis Felder.

Dr. Felder expressed genuine interest in my plans. He had a soft voice that spoke sincerely and a personal, almost intimate manner.

"You'll never regret going to graduate school. You've chosen a good profession to enter."

"I didn't choose it. It chose me, and I'm scared to death I won't pass. It's been fourteen years since I finished college."

"I know how you feel. After my wife and I had three children and I had established a general practice, I went back to school."

"Really?"

"Yes. We had to sell our home and uproot the whole family. It wasn't easy."

"I have three children, too," I offered, feeling a camaraderie of spirit. "What did you study?"

"Internal medicine. I wanted to specialize."

By the time I left his office, Louis Felder had become my friend.

Before I received my official acceptance in Emory's graduate school, I asked my closest friends to pray that nothing would hinder my getting in and doing the Lord's will. After the admittance letters arrived, it was fun to share the news. The summer took on a special glow of happiness and promise and I seized every opportunity to make extra money.

Sue and Sydney were called to audition for the Chemstrand company. They wanted two adult models and two children. Buyers from nationally known stores were to fly in for a special showing of sports clothes made of a new fabric. The models, wearing stretch pants and bathing suits, would demonstrate, by doing exercises, and diving in the pool and swimming, that the colors were equally pretty wet or dry and the dye was fast.

Mrs. Woodley, the company representative, selected Sue and Sydney to be the child models. I assured her they were excellent swimmers. She measured them and called me when the clothes came in from the factory.

"Will you bring the girls over? I'm sure the clothes will fit, but I'd rather check."

When we arrived, Mrs. Woodley was talking on the telephone, obviously upset. I couldn't help hearing her part of the conversation.

"Miss Lyon, this is the most unethical proposal I've ever heard. We agreed on salary when models were auditioned."

After a pause she continued.

"This show is extremely important to our organization. We want the best models in Atlanta and have offered the top fee. I consider your conduct at this date outrageous. I will not raise the fee, and, furthermore, we will not need your services at all!"

That finalized, she turned her attention to us, offering an explanation.

"Some of these younger girls are so greedy. I'd hired the two models at twenty dollars an hour, as you know, and at the eleventh hour they're demanding more."

"How could they do that?"

"They probably got together and assumed I'd pay it, having ordered their sizes. I hate it when people deliberately try to take advantage. Chemstrand is a generous company and I'm paying the top price, but I won't use that girl, now or ever, even if I'm a model short."

"You have every right to be upset."

"Miss Lyon said they should be paid more for getting their hair wet swimming!"

I laughed! "That is funny. I swim every time I get a chance for nothing. What fun to do it for twenty dollars an hour!"

"You know most of these models. Do you know Miss Lyon?" Mrs. Woodley asked me.

"Oh, yes. We're not friends, but I see her a lot. She is much in demand as a fashion model. Funny, she and I wear the same size dress though she's much taller."

It took a lot of nerve for me to say that!

Mrs. Woodley looked at me with a gleam in her eye. "Stand up," she ordered.

"Oh, I couldn't," I answered, rising. "I'm not a fashion model."

"You're shorter, but your figure is better. You're well-rounded, and buyers like that."

"But the other girl is a head taller than I am. We'd look terrible together," I said, hoping she wouldn't agree.

"Contrast is good. It will show the versatility of the design and the stretch fabric's adaptability. Besides, I'd much rather give you the money. You've been cooperative. Try these on."

They fit perfectly!

Thank You, Lord.

Mrs. Woodley appeared calm and pleased at the turnout the morning of the show. She estimated that two hundred or more prospective buyers were gathered around the pool. Just before our entrance, she spoke to the other adult model and me.

"After the exercises, Sally, you dive in with the children and swim. Mrs. Stewart's hair is too pretty to get wet. Suzanne, you walk around the side of the pool for the photographers."

What irony. I didn't dare look at Sally for fear I'd laugh. She must be furious.

When we were all back in the dressing room later, Sally dressed quickly, hardly drying her hair. Mrs. Woodley paid her without a word and she left. Then the atmosphere changed immediately.

"Suzanne, I'm very pleased with the show. You were lovely, and your daughters adorable. They're so winsome. I appreciate how easy you are to work with and your effort to make this successful. In addition to the money, I'd like to give you all the clothes."

"My goodness!" I exclaimed. "Girls, did you hear that?"

"Thank you, Mrs. Woodley. I love mine!" Sue said happily.

Sydney shyly gave Mrs. Woodley a hug.

"And I'd like to invite you to stay for the luncheon.

You don't have to, of course, but I'd like to have you meet some of the people here. They might like to ask you questions—your reaction to the clothes."

"Oh, mama, please stay," Sydney pleaded.

"We'd love to," I answered. "This will be an extra treat."

Lord, how dear are the people you bring into our lives! Money, clothes, fun, food, and a new friend. You are a morale booster! All this, and not a hair out of place!

23

Clay Feet

"We're supposed to register at Emory in a few days, Dr. McCroskey, and I don't know what to do. I haven't received the tuition money you offered. Do you pay the school directly or what?"

I had had no communication from Dr. McCroskey since my acceptance. With registration just a few days away, I became concerned and called him.

"Oh, yes, I did promise you a grant, didn't I," he said cordially. "Well, let me tell you what happened."

As he paused, I felt the familiar tightening of my stomach muscles and my heart beat faster. Bad news was coming!

"I had a letter from a lady in Texas asking about the program," Dr. McCroskey explained. "She is a natural for Speech and Hearing. She has a degree in education, five years' teaching experience, and wants the challenge of special education."

He paused again. I felt anxiety and confusion. Why was he telling me this?

"She needed a little persuasion to quit her job and move across country. I had to offer her the scholarship money. We couldn't afford to lose her."

We were both silent. I struggled to adjust, but the shock of his words staggered me!

"Mrs. Stewart? Mrs. Stewart, are you there?"

"Dr. McCroskey, are you saying you gave the lady from Texas *my* money?"

"She has outstanding qualifications. There's no doubt she'll be an asset in our profession."

Don't tell me how great she is, I wanted to scream at him. Fighting to control the tears of frustration and disappointment sure to come, I replied, "But that money wasn't yours to give. You *had given* it to me. That money was sanctified—set apart."

"Mrs. Stewart, apparently you don't see—"

"No, I don't," I interrupted. "You've done a terrible thing, and you had no right to do it. You can't promise a person something that will change her life, cause her to make plans for herself and her family, and then excuse it by 'a lady from Texas came along'!"

The tears surfaced.

"Dr. McCroskey, I must hang up. Good-by."

"Now wait a minute. Let's talk this thing over. Maybe we can work something out."

"I can't talk any longer. Don't you realize what you've done?"

"Let's talk. There might be a solution."

"I can't. I'm going to cry. Forgive me if I'm rude, but I must hang up. Good-by."

My self-control broke, I wept bitterly. Stretched out across the bed, I pounded the mattress with my fist.

How could he? How could he? How could he?

And I cried.

It was my money. My scholarship. What difference does it make who came along?

And I cried.

Time passed. Perhaps an hour.

"It will be all right," the voice said.

I know. I know You wouldn't let anything happen unless it was best for me. I know that. I just wanted to go so badly.

"You will."

Then why this shock?

"You haven't yet learned to trust Me. You reacted emotionally. I've told you to thank Me in all things. Cast out your fears. I plan your steps. Rely on it. What you see, hear, or feel may have nothing to do with what is true. Trust Me."

Calmed, but sad, I rose and washed my face, wondering how I could tell mother and my friends.

The telephone rang. I knew it would be Dr. McCroskey.

"Hello."

"Suzanne, this is Bob McCroskey. Now don't hang up. I've made a few calls, and it looks as if we'll have some money for you."

He's tried, I thought. He's done his best to make amends.

"Suzanne, are you there?"

"Yes."

"Won't six hundred dollars get you started? I've managed to raise that."

Half a loaf is better than none, and that's more than

half. Still, something valuable was gone—lost forever. Something worth more than money.

"Yes," I said. "I guess so."

"Okay then! I'll be in my office on campus registration day. You report to me first. We'll make out your schedule and pay the fees."

"Thank you."

"Everything will turn out all right."

As always, he sounded cheerful.

"Yes. Thank you. Good-by."

What a sad way to start such a wonderful new adventure—disillusioned with the man I saw as the most important person in it.

The inner voice chided me. "You expect people to be perfect. They aren't. You want to idolize a human being. You mustn't. It is better for you to realize, in the beginning, that Dr. McCroskey is human—weak, as all humans are. Otherwise you could worship him."

I would ponder those words a long, long time.

24

College Was Never Like This

FALL QUARTER INFORMATION surrounded me like leaves swirling in the wind. There seemed no end of terms to learn because each class had its own vocabulary. I felt like a stranger in a foreign land. Fundamentals were essential and difficult for me to grasp. Half the time I didn't understand what was being said. How could I discover what it meant? Each course required its own outside reading materials. I couldn't believe so much was expected of us!

The first class I attended was Teaching of the Deaf taught by Miss Evans. The group sat around a large library table. As she talked, the other students wrote. How rude, I thought, for them not to give her the courtesy of attention. I was the only one who looked at her.

"What were you writing during class?" I asked the girl next to me.

"I was taking notes, and you'd better, too, if you expect to pass!"

Clearly my idea of graduate school needed revising. I'd have to learn how to study. I discovered my expectations were as childish as other romantic fantasies. I thought everything we learned would be recorded in textbooks. Not so! The lectures included much additional information. Thinking classes would take just three or four hours a day, I expected to have as much, or more, time at home as when I'd worked at Fritz Orr. In reality, we were required to observe all the classes taught at the Atlanta Speech School, which took several hours a day. We were even scheduled to visit other special education schools, clinics, and hospitals during Thanksgiving holidays. We used the library during any free time.

Housework suffered neglect and laundry piled high. Nights were no longer my own. Monday nights we observed the adult classes in lip-reading, stuttering, and voice. Tuesday nights there was an education course on the Emory campus.

I surely hadn't known what I was getting into!

Dr. McCroskey's cheerfulness and sense of humor kept me balanced. No matter how fearful, depressed, or weary I became, I responded positively to his good disposition.

There were many people to become acquainted with now: the large staff at the Atlanta Speech School, the children who attended regularly, Emory professors and secretaries, and my fellow students.

Eleven of us began the program in the fall. Two older women were teachers on leave of absence from the Atlanta Public Schools. One of them quit the first month. Two others were mothers of deaf children who were students at the Speech School. Five were young women just out of college earning a higher degree. Then, of course, there was that lady from Texas. And me.

It took me awhile to discover that there were a few other students. They had been in the program the year before but had not yet completed all the requirements. Some, like Jerry, a part-time staff audiologist, worked and attended a few courses.

The obvious caste system shocked me! Staff was staff. Students were students. We were allowed to eat in the staff dining room, but we weren't included in their conversations.

Perhaps my biggest personal crisis came one Monday during one of those lunch periods.

"You should have heard my minister yesterday," Dr. McCroskey said. "He didn't have three sentences in his sermon relating to one another. He's cracking up. Not once did he tie anything up to the announced topic. He was further from the subject than I am from the presidency."

The students were silent, but staff members laughed. I became tense and uncomfortable.

"He couldn't have been further out on cloud nine. He said. . . ."

I tuned him out for a minute.

Lord, help me. Dr. McCroskey is poking fun at one of Your servants. Should I leave and say nothing?

"The man is going bananas," Dr. McCroskey continued.

Lord, they're laughing at his imitation. I don't want to get in this. I like Dr. McCroskey. He's my only friend here. If I take issue with him, I may ruin any chance I have of succeeding in graduate school.

The inner voice said, "It's up to you. If you feel you must, take the chance."

I tuned back in to Dr. McCroskey.

"The congregation didn't know whether to laugh or cry. The man is nuts."

"You're not helping him any by your comments," I blurted, more harshly than I intended.

"What did you say, Mrs. Stewart?"

I took a deep breath.

"I said you're not helping him. If you care, you should pray for him."

"The man is beyond help, Mrs. Stewart. He's obviously having a nervous breakdown."

"All the more reason he needs your love and support, not your ridicule."

The clatter of plates, forks, and spoons died away. The room could have been empty, it was so quiet. Acutely self-conscious, I *knew* I'd caused the tension. Dr. McCroskey's tone of voice reflected only interest in my statements, no criticism or resentment. The hushed quietness indicated that everyone else was uncomfortable, or perhaps eager to witness whatever was about to happen.

Miss Rogers, one of my teachers, stared at me as if I had lost my mind.

Oh, Lord, she and I already have a personality conflict. This won't help a bit. I know she's unsympathetic with my views.

"I didn't realize you felt so strongly, Mrs. Stewart. Do you know my minister?"

"No, but I know many other ministers. They need our loyalty. All of them are under great strain and pressure. The Bible tells us to pray for those over us spiritually."

"This man has lost the ability to lead."

"It is still your responsibility to remain loyal. He needs the support of his congregation. Your prayers could help."

"I see. Very interesting, Mrs. Stewart."

He turned to another member of the staff and addressed a question on a different subject. Our conversation was closed.

I felt sick. No one spoke to me as we left the room and returned to class.

Lord, was I wrong to speak?

The answer came a few hours later through a younger student, Judy Williams. Judy was jolly and friendly and liked by all. In the ladies' room she whispered, "I'm so glad you said what you did at lunch. I wanted to say something but didn't have the nerve. My father is a minister. I know how they suffer and sacrifice! I knew just how you felt."

In addition to the pressures at school, there were many at home. I, who hated confusion, had to live in disorderly surroundings. There was no way to keep things clean and straight. Often I became irritable with the children, only to be beseiged with guilt later. They were so young and I was unbearably cross. Occasionally Lettie would come over, bringing her rug shampooer, floor waxer, and other equipment, and clean and scrub until her back hurt. I could never do that for anyone, I thought with shame.

Doris Boggs, who often kept Hunt in the afternoons, volunteered to do my laundry!

"Now, Suzanne, I want to have a part in your attending graduate school. I can't help you with money, but I can do this. I've a washing machine and dryer that really do the work, and I like to iron. It will give me something to do while I'm watching television at night, and I won't feel guilty. Frank's out of town so much on his concert tours, and the girls go to bed early, so this is the best way for me to contribute."

My friends and my mother gave practical help beyond my imagination. It humbled me to see such love in action.

Finances were still a constant problem. The National Defense Student Loan provided for awhile, but I couldn't do the odd jobs I'd planned because of the lack of time.

Surprises came. I opened a letter from an aunt in Florida and two much-handled five dollar bills fell out. She had told her egg man, a Christian lay preacher, about my faith and situation and had asked him to pray for me. He said he would and gave her the money to send to me!

A friend I'd known since college sent me a typewriter! He said, "You can't get a master's degree without one."

My milkman never worried when my bill ran high. He assured me he knew it would be paid in time and "not to worry—keep studying."

At the end of fall quarter, Nan, a fellow student, invited me to bring the children for Sunday dinner at her apartment.

Nan had come from Macon, Georgia, with her sons, Martin, Jr. and Tony, who was deaf. An infant daughter stayed in Macon in Nan's sister's care. Nan's husband, Martin, remained there, too, because of his work. A civic club was paying Nan's expenses in order to have a citizen in Macon who could teach a class for the deaf.

"Oh, Nan, there are too many of us."

"No, I'm used to cooking for large crowds at home. Martin will be here. We especially want all of you. Please come."

On Sunday we sat down to a marvelous dinner of fried chicken, rice, vegetables, and homemade rolls!

After the blessing, Nan said, "We want to ask a big favor of you."

"What?"

I felt a touch of resentment and suspicion that I'd been invited for a purpose, but quickly squelched it. Nan's trusting blue eyes met mine, and I was impressed by her simple honesty. She was the kind of woman who provided strength for her family by example, inspiration, and encouragement.

"The club sponsoring me doesn't have enough money to keep us in this apartment anymore. I know you're a real Christian. You've had a tough time financially, too, and can understand our predicament. We wondered if you'd let the boys and me live at your house next quarter?"

My mind whirled in surprise at the sudden proposal. Other than the summer with Jenny, we had never had an outsider living with us. But the house was big enough. The upstairs hadn't been used since I'd had a live-in maid.

Lord, it's Your house. Is it to shelter this family, too?

"Maybe we could pay you a little rent?" Martin offered, breaking the silence.

"No," I answered quickly. "I couldn't charge you. The Lord provided the house. He'd want me to share it. I just don't know if you could stand it. We're living completely by faith. I don't have any income, and we hardly know what will happen from day to day. There's no one to keep house. The children are too young to help much so things stay in a mess. You're welcome to come, but you should know what you're getting into."

"I could help with the food and utilities," Nan suggested hopefully.

"That would be nice. Perhaps this is God's way of helping us both through school."

And so it was decided.

Before school dismissed for the Christmas holidays, Dr. McCroskey teased us pleasantly, "I want to wish you all a Merry Christmas. For those of you who flunk out, if any, Happy New Year. If you are concerned about a grade in one of my classes, leave a self-addressed postcard with me. I'll send your grade as soon as the exam is graded and scores totaled. This will reach you several days before your official record comes through the Emory office."

The postcard I left with him arrived just before Christmas. It had a big "P" for "passed" on it and a "Merry Christmas."

25

Overconfident

WINTER QUARTER PASSED swiftly—perhaps because I had Nan to share it with me. We did more than study and work together. We prayed together! There was so little money, so many children, and so much need. Books alone cost over fifty dollars a quarter.

Dr. Broyles, who was concerned about us, sent Jenny Pope to see me. She said he thought I'd speak more openly to a woman. And I did I guess. Jenny must have told him there was no food in the refrigerator, for he sent me three hundred dollars.

Bless his heart! He cared for us with devotion both spiritual and material. I hoped all the sheep in his flock hadn't been as troublesome as I.

Nan never showed a sign of nerves. She always spoke gently to the children, even in disciplining. I appreciated the patience she exhibited while helping my little Sue learn her multiplication tables.

Having a deaf child in the house was an education! Typically, Tony's actions were abnormally loud. Sometimes during car rides and mealtimes I thought I'd scream when the noise reached such a high volume. He banged things together. Because his speech was limited, he vocalized babblings and odd noises constantly.

I finally resorted to earplugs and wore them for weeks without the other members of the household knowing. Not only did it cut the noise, but it also sharpened my lip-reading ability.

The best thing about the term was an Audiology course taught by Mr. Greene. He was a stickler for facts, but once you had learned something in his class, you didn't forget it.

Nan, being very studious, drilled me nightly. Often she'd prod my shoulder to keep me awake.

"Leave me alone, Nan. I've just got to go to bed. I'm so sleepy."

Sweetly she tolerated all my protests, but relentlessly continued asking me questions. "Define auditory agnosia. Pillars of Carti. Dysacusis. What is a threshold shift? How is a diagnosis of otosclerosis made? Locate the ossicles. Eustachian tube. Footplate of the stapes."

She wouldn't let me go to bed until I gave the right answers, and we made two of the highest grades on a difficult mid-term.

Once a week I gave hearing tests at Grady Hospital as part of the Audiology course. The otologist there praised my work and said he'd like to hire me. I wondered if he had the influence or power to do so. When I got sick a few days later, I found out he couldn't even get me an aspirin!

I continued working that day, feeling worse every hour. The testing booths were small and very hot. Finally I left the hospital. By the time I arrived home, my fever was raging. Dr. Felder had to be called to the house that night. As he leaned over and spoke to me, I felt too far away to answer, but his presence helped. I believed he'd get me well.

The flu I had was highly contagious. Dr. Felder thought

it easier to isolate me in my bedroom in the far wing of the house than in a hospital.

For the next two days mother and Nan bore all the responsibilities. On Friday Nan and the boys went home to Macon for the weekend, while mother nursed me and took care of the children. The anti-toxins worked and I was up by Sunday, though very weak.

Should I go to the Speech School on Monday and take the final exam in Audiology? Mr. Greene would have to make out an entirely new test for me if I missed the one given on exam day. I'd missed Friday's lecture, and with Nan gone, there was no way to get the information. My mid-term, hospital work, and daily grades would give me a high average. We were graded on the "EGPU" system —Excellent, Good, Passing, Unsatisfactory. Passing meant a score of eighty to ninety. I didn't want to be extra trouble for Mr. Greene so I decided to chance taking the exam. It could only mean the difference between "G" and "P."

Monday morning I spoke to Mr. Greene as we entered the library.

"You know I've had a bad case of the flu and missed Friday's lecture? Will that affect my exam much? I haven't had time to borrow anyone's notes. Should I wait and take the exam later?"

"No, take it now."

Later that week I had a rare opportunity to earn money. After finishing the early morning job, I rushed to the school for my final exam in Lip-Reading. There was a notice in my mailbox to see Miss Rogers when it was over.

"Mrs. Stewart, I want to discuss your Stuttering grade with you," she said when I got there.

We'd had no tests or exams in her class.

"I don't feel right about passing you."

"Well, I certainly won't feel good if you don't," I smiled. She couldn't be serious.

"On what grounds do you feel you should pass?"

"Well, I've attended every class, except one last week when I was sick. I've finished all the assignments and outside work, haven't I?"

"Yes. What I question is your understanding of the problem. I don't think you do."

"I've learned all the experts opinions—six entirely different theories. There is a question of their understanding the problem," I chuckled.

"Yes, but their professional standing is established. Yours is not."

"Well, I've enjoyed the class. If there was anything I failed to do, I don't know it."

"We have a responsibility to see that a person does more than assimilate knowledge. A therapist must use it correctly. I'm not sure you would."

I now felt decidedly uneasy.

Lord, what is she up to? What game is she playing? Cat and mouse?

"I'm wondering, Mrs. Stewart, if you can give me any reason to pass you?"

Lord, she wants me to beg her! I think she wants me to sit here, sniffle and cry, so she can end up being Lady Bountiful.

I stood, ready to leave the presence of this woman. A sick one, in my opinion.

"Miss Rogers, each of us has problems every day. Somehow we all have to do the best we can. Today, I've dressed, fed, and cared for three children, worked in two fashion shows, and taken a graduate school final examination. It's not yet noon. I've done the best I can so far with my day and plan to continue doing so. I trust you'll do your best with yours."

It wasn't just an exit line. I really believed her professional ethics ensured her doing the right thing when she thought it over.

Talk about a "cockeyed optimist"—Rodgers and Hammerstein should have known me! I had a lot to learn.

26

Get the Nuts out of the Program

Mr. Greene and I almost collided. I was running up the steps of the Speech School on the first day of spring quarter, happy to be back.

After my apology for clumsiness, he said, "Say, I bet your Audiology grade really surprised you."

"I haven't received my grades yet." I must have gotten a "G", I thought, pleased.

"You mean Emory hasn't mailed them?"

"Guess not. Mine haven't come."

"But everyone's registered. Classes start today."

"Right! Let's get the show on the road." I really felt good. Such a contrast to the week before.

"Then you don't know?"

"Know what?"

"I failed you."

"You're kidding."

"No, I did. Your final was terrible."

My vitality and bounce disappeared.

"When I saw that one of the five questions was on the last lecture, I knew twenty points was lost."

"You missed other things, too. Come by my office and we'll go over your paper."

"That's all right. I know you grade accurately. I don't need to see it." I needed to be alone.

"Come on. I want to go over it with you."

If it was done, it was done. His grades were recorded at Emory, too late to change. There was no point in asking why he hadn't averaged in my high marks. Why make him feel badly?

We spent half an hour going over the exam. He'd taken points off for all sorts of little things. Minus two here, minus one there, and it added up to a failure. He explained every mark logically, and I nodded in agreement. Poor man. He justified the "U" but seemed unhappy. I felt sorry for him.

Before the morning ended, I found I'd overestimated Miss Rogers too. She failed me, as she'd suggested she would. And of all things, I had signed up to take Mental Hygiene from her this quarter.

I went to classes as usual. A few days later a note asking me to report to Dr. McCroskey's office came as no surprise. We were supposed to maintain a passing average in all subjects to remain in graduate school. I could guess what would happen since I had failed two!

I vaguely remembered something about being required to reimburse the Speech School tuition money in case of failure. That meant I owed them one hundred and fifty dollars!

I knocked on his door.

"I'm tied up for a few minutes, Mrs. Stewart. Please wait in the library until I send for you," Dr. McCroskey answered.

The library was empty.

Lord, don't let me disgrace You. I'm sorry I failed. Just don't let me fail as a Christian!

This interview with Dr. McCroskey is going to be difficult. If I'm to be like You, I can't speak against

*Miss Rogers or Mr. Greene. Neither can I defend
myself. That doesn't leave much for me to say.*

"Leave that to me. Don't worry. Spend your time
profitably. Relax. Read."

*I'm not in the mood for scientific journals, but I'll
do whatever You say.*

I scanned the monthly literature and selected a psychology magazine. An article on maturity caught my
eye. Settling down in an easy chair, I read with real
interest. At the end was a ten-point test of maturity.

That's really good, I decided, and copied it word for
word on paper in my clipboard.

When Dr. McCroskey came to get me, he said nothing
until we had entered his office and closed the door.

"Sit down, Suzanne. I hope you realize we're in a very
bad predicament."

"You mean about my failing my favorite courses last
quarter?" I smiled.

"Yes."

"It is a nuisance." I tried to sound lighthearted.

"It may be a great deal more than a nuisance. It may
well be the end of your graduate school career."

"Why?"

"Dean Randall has called several times for an explanation. He wants me to justify keeping you in the program."

"I hope you can," I said softly and seriously.

"I told him about your having the flu just before the
Audiology exam. It's a bit harder to explain your failure
in Stuttering."

"Yes, it is difficult to explain flunking a course with no
exam." I had let a little bitterness creep into my voice.

"That's not the point. A teacher has every right to grade on the merit of the individual."

"Agreed. I wish they would."

We sat in silence, seemingly getting nowhere.

"Is that all you have to say about it?" Dr. McCroskey asked.

"What can I say to you? You know all the people involved. I expect you've checked the facts pretty accurately."

"You bet I have! We've had more staff meetings over you than any student who has ever been here!"

"Oh? I didn't know I was such a celebrity."

"Fall quarter you were the prime subject of our weekly staffings. The majority were for washing you out then. No one understands what makes you tick. I find your attitude a bit bizarre myself."

"Because I don't weep, wail, and moan? Get angry or retaliate?"

"You could show a little more emotion about failing two subjects and getting kicked out of graduate school."

"I can't equate the two things. One hasn't even happened. I'm certainly not embarrassed by the failures, though I regret them. I know as much about Audiology as anyone else in the class. Get the exam or make up one and test me yourself."

"What about the other failure? I talked to Miss Rogers. She said you were called in to discuss it and made no effort to pass. She tried to help you, she said, and you walked out. Is that true?"

"Dr. McCroskey," I cocked my head to one side and said daringly, "you'll just have to choose between Miss Rogers and me. One of us has got to go."

"I beg your pardon?" He had a "did I hear you right" expression on his face.

"She is definitely an obstacle in my path. I've tried to

get around her, over, and under. I'm blocked. You'll have to choose between us." I spoke intensely. I meant it.

"Inasmuch as she's been here for twenty-five years and you're a student in questionable status, the choice will hardly be difficult."

He was serious, too. I was disappointed and reverted to flippancy.

"Then you'll never know what you missed."

We retreated into silence again. I felt angry with my professors for causing this scene. Apparently Dr. McCroskey was being put through an ordeal by his superiors. I'd never known him to fail in matching my humor, and I missed his delightful, upbeat voice.

Oh, Lord, help him. How awful for his loyalties to be divided. He is such a fine man and wants to be fair. Help him. Help me.

Much to my surprise, he took the Audiology exam out of my folder and began questioning me. I gave him the correct answers, even the one on the last lecture. I'd studied Nan's notes on it, preparing for the advanced course in Audiology this quarter.

When we finished, Dr. McCroskey sighed deeply.

"Dean Randall told me to get the nuts out of the program."

We were quiet for another moment while I digested that. Then I sighed deeply.

"Dr. McCroskey, you do believe in scientific evidence, don't you?"

"Of course I do."

"Then let me ask you ten questions, formulated after much research. They're on maturity. Will you keep me in mind and answer them honestly? Then decide if you think I'm a nut."

"Shoot."

I started down the list before me. Not only did my behavior seem more and more mature with each question, but some of the other people who came to my mind began to compare with monkeys. Infants, anyway.

When we reached the end, I could see those eyes twinkling once more.

"Where did you get that?" he asked.

"Out of one of the journals in your library."

"While you were waiting for me?"

"That's right."

He stared at me intently as if I weren't real, "You just happened to read it?"

"Yes, sir."

"And why did you copy it?"

"I don't know. It appealed to me and I wanted to have it."

"It has come in handy!"

I waited, not knowing what to say.

He grinned the most infectious grin I've ever seen.

"Mrs. Stewart, you do have something, or Someone, special going for you! I'll speak to Dean Randall. But from now on—*no more failures*."

"*Yes, sir!*"

27

How Long Until Daybreak?

Lord, I'm in such pain!

Fitfully I tossed from one side of the bed to the other. My stomach hurt dreadfully. Sharp pains came at irregular intervals.

Oh, Lord, help me through this night.

Money. What would we do? I had no money. Broke again. What had I done in the past? Nothing. Just believed the Lord would provide. My daily needs had to come through God's resources, not mine.

How had that dear Mary Kate Duskin found out about me? She was treasurer of the Altrusa Club. I'd never heard of it before she called me.

"One of our members, Alice Rivers, goes to your church. She told us what a wonderful thing you're doing in studying speech therapy, but she said you need financial help. Our club has a scholarship account to lend money to those who are endeavoring to further their education. We're interested in helping you."

"Oh, Miss Duskin, how wonderful! You don't know how badly I need it!"

"Suppose we start by sending you two hundred dollars?

Perhaps later we can add to this amount if you need it."

"I'd be grateful! This comes at a time when I need money badly."

"Good. We want our funds to be in use. Later on when you're at work, you can repay the account and we'll have it to help someone else."

Miss Duskin is really nice. She was sweet to meet me on the campus for dinner. I think her interest is sincere. She'll call me again. I'll borrow more from the Altrusa Club if it's necessary.

Oh, this pain. Maybe the heating pad would help. But what if it's appendicitis? I should use ice.

Oh, Lord, tell me what to do.

Bills are so high. I'm still getting high heat bills, though it's spring. Lights. Water. Food. That registered letter!

They're so frightening, Lord. Almost always bad news.

Lovett's treasurer, Mr. Rabbe, didn't know how upset I'd get when he wrote about the girls' tuition. He probably was trying to help by suggesting I take them out at mid-term and put them in public school.

"I can't, Mr. Rabbe. Don't you see? They've been here for years—more than half their lifetime. They started in nursery school, and Sue's in fourth grade now, Sydney in second. With all the moves we've made in and out of our house, this school and our church have been their security. Homes, of a sort. It would be terrible to change schools in the middle of the year. Please let them stay. They've had so many adjustments to make. I'll take them out next year. My work at Emory will be completed, and I will probably be employed by the school system. I'd feel peculiar earning money in the public schools and sending them to private school anyway. That would be the natural time for them to change.

"Just let them finish this year here. Please. You know I'll pay you, no matter how long it takes."

Lord, why can't I forget? That's past. Mr. Rabbe agreed. Why do I keep thinking about it? Please put me to sleep.

Maybe a pillow under my stomach and sleeping face down would help.

Joe.

; Thank You, Father, for Joe.

Even though it's been almost two years since I left the welfare department, he still calls every few months to see how we are.

Father, I have trusted in You to provide. I've never asked anyone for a dime.

Joe always asked just the right questions to ferret out my problems. He was very specific. Months ago when he'd determined that I was worried about unpaid utility bills, he'd asked the exact amount owed each and added it up. He had then sent me a check for the total sum.

God, thank You for providing such friends.

I'll bet Joe and his wife only have high school educations. Amazing that they care about my getting through graduate school! That's true Christian love. Like what he'd done for us a few days ago—just before I'd registered for this quarter.

"Suzanne, Bea and I have been praying for you."

"I know, Joe. Keep it up."

"How are things going?"

"About the same."

"Do you have the tuition money for next quarter?"

"No."

"Any prospects for getting it?"

"No."

"Good!"

"Good? Joe, you're crazy!"

"Yes, good! Otherwise Bea and I might be getting the wrong message. You see, I inherited a little money. Not much, but useful. Bea and I don't really need it now. Of course, we may someday. We decided we would rather invest it in the Lord's work than banks. How would you like us to send you—say six hundred dollars?"

I couldn't believe my ears!

"That would pay your spring tuition, buy books, and groceries for awhile."

"Joe, I don't know what to say."

"Nothing necessary. The Lord provides."

Oh, Lord, what if I should fail again?

Lettie got the money from her sister to give me a hundred and fifty dollars to repay the Speech School. Her husband would have objected to her using his money in this way.

At least I made "G" on my other subjects. That ought to prove something. I did better than pass. Nobody but a research genius ever makes "E."

*Father, I'm dying. How long must I wait to call Dr.
Felder? I can't wake him, can I?*

Debts. Debts. Debts.

I'm building a mountain of debts. How will I ever
repay so much money?

Lucy. How much do I owe Lucy? She offered to lend
me the money to go to the Southern Speech Association
Convention in Nashville. Dr. McCroskey urged us to
go now that we know enough to understand the lectures.

I try not to neglect Lucy. I don't mind stopping by for
short visits after church. Retired people must get very
lonely. She's sweet to the children. Letting them lick the
envelopes and stamp her Christmas cards as a "job"—two
dollars apiece for their Christmas shopping money. Well,
she knows how much I owe her. Lucy keeps records.

Oh, mercy! I *hurt.*

Lord, why do I have such pain?

It's as bad as going to the dentist!

The dentist. Why, oh why, did I get so upset about our
teeth last fall? None of us had been to a dentist in three
years, but couldn't we have waited one more? I brooded
until Doris Boggs discovered it bothered me terribly. She
talked to a friend of hers who agreed to do our work and
wait for payments until after I finished school.

The dentist admired my efforts, he said. He would like
to have someone with my Christian character working in
his office.

Now I owed him almost four hundred dollars.

*Lord, it's too much. I'll never get through. Even if I
do, I'll never get out of debt.*

I looked at the clock. What time is dawn? Doctors rise early. Surely it would be all right to call Dr. Felder at 6:30 A.M.

Pains gripped me.

I can't wait that long, Lord.

Maybe 6:00 A.M.

Shoes. We all need shoes. It seems to me someone always needs shoes. I've got to get shoes for the children before Easter.

What is left to sell? Why did I lose so much that could have been sold?

Father, forgive me, but I do miss my oriental rugs and dining room furniture more than anything.

My most valuable earrings—gone. Lost at Grady Hospital while giving hearing tests. Lost or stolen.

Who but a fool would wear them in the daytime?

Well, everyone thought they were rhinestones.

Mother's said a thousand times, "Jewelry is to be worn. Never take rings off your fingers except for cleaning."

That goes for earrings too. I shouldn't have removed them.

Father, I can't stand it much longer. Please make the dawn come.

What will I do this summer? I won't be able to ride with Nan. She'll take the boys back to Macon when their school term ends. Then she'll rent a room closer to the Speech School.

Oh, Lord, is that sunlight?

I dialed Dr. Felder.

The minute he answered, hot, salty tears started rolling down my cheeks.

"Oh, Dr. Felder, this is Suzanne. I'm sick again. Stomach pains. I've been awake all night."

"Do you have any fever?" he asked.

"No; I don't think so. Just awful pains. Do you think its appendicitis?"

I answered all his questions. Then he advised me.

"Suzanne, it's nothing to be alarmed about. I know you're suffering, but we can relieve the pain. It's caused by nerves. You're living under a tremendous emotional strain and something was bound to happen. You may even have more attacks like this, but once you're through school and living a more normal life, they'll stop. Now tell me the name of a drugstore near you and I'll call in a prescription."

"They wouldn't be open out here for a long time. It's Sunday. I've got to get up and take the children to Sunday school."

"I'll phone it in to Marshall and Bell's. You can pick it up there and go on to church."

So I began a pattern repeated often through the next two years. As Dr. Felder said, the attacks recurred. What he didn't predict: they were always on Saturday night! When I "relaxed from the week."

What a way to relax!

28

A Personality for Posterity

"How's YOUR THESIS moving along? Something about stuttering, isn't it?" Dr. McCroskey asked, as he opened the windows of his office.

"Yes. I'm not making much progress."

"You don't care much for scientific research, do you?" he observed seriously.

"No. I'd rather let others do it."

He leaned forward, one foot propped on a small bookshelf, arms crossed over his knees. His head almost touched the window screen, and he listened intently to the children on the playground below. It wasn't just deaf children he liked to hear. I'd observed him, while a passenger in his car, lowering the window whenever passing through a school zone. Dr. McCroskey never minded sacrificing air-conditioned comfort for the pleasures of hearing laughter. Wonderful man. Few people see and hear their environment.

"I've been doing a lot of thinking about you, Mrs. Stewart."

"Oh?" I was puzzled and slightly uneasy.

"It seems I spend a lot of time worrying about you. You've kept me awake at night."

"Sometimes you have to lose sleep to solve a problem," I said lightly.

"I think we were wrong in our treatment of you. There's no point in trying to fit a square peg in a round hole."

"I'm a square?" I teased.

"Yes. Instead of trying to make you fit the image we had of a student, we should have looked at the unique things you could bring into our profession." He closed the windows and took a seat opposite me. "I have an idea."

"What?" I prodded.

"You like to write. You scored high on the English and General Culture exams. The whole staff has noticed your lengthy reports and attention to recorded details of your cases." He paused momentarily. "Why don't you scratch the work you've done toward your thesis and start over? *You* could do a literary project."

My heart pounded as it always did in response to an exciting idea or possibility. It might be from God!

"We've never had a literary project done in our department. You could write the first!"

My nature responded easily to the thought of doing something special. I loved being different.

"What could I write about?" I asked hesitantly. Strange that my outer communication at such times never revealed the inner excitement.

"Edith Fitzgerald! Write a biography of Edith Fitzgerald."

A sinking sensation filled me. Dr. McCroskey's idea was too big! Deaf herself, Edith Fitzgerald had created the Fitzgerald Key, a method of teaching language to the deaf which was used internationally.

"You mean a book of her life?" I asked dumbly. "But she's the most famous teacher of the deaf, except Alexander Graham Bell."

"On the contrary. Very little is known about her,

except her contribution to the deaf. There is no real record of her life."

"I don't think I could do it. It certainly should be written, but not by me. It's too big. A real writer should do it."

"I believe you can write it. It has never been done because the right person hadn't come along. I think you're that person." He leaned back with his hands behind his head, looking completely confident and relaxed.

My heart began beating faster. His assurance almost erased my doubts. "How would I get the information?"

"Interviews with people who knew her, letters, public records, a few trips. You should visit the Georgia School for the Deaf. Miss Fitzgerald spent her last working years there. Marie Kinnard, who is still there, probably would be your best source of information. They collaborated on some writings. This is an entirely different type of research work, but one you should enjoy."

"It might take years to do all that. I couldn't possibly finish it by August."

"No, I don't think that would be possible. You'd have to give up your dream of graduating at that time."

He glanced over and met my eyes. I felt I was being tested. "But I have to go to work. I have to!" My voice was almost a whisper.

"You could get a job with the school system without a master's. They wouldn't pay as much, of course. You have to be fully certified after one year, but they will take a person with a "provisional" certificate. You'd be eligible for that."

"My mother and friends would be so disappointed."

"Not unless you are. It's no disgrace to take two years to complete a master's program. After this year it will be set up that way. We're revamping the program completely."

"At least I'd be doing a thesis I'd like."

"If you do it well, and you'll have to for it to be accepted, your family and friends ought to be very proud of you. Writing a biography is not an everyday thing."

Lord, I know this is from You. It has to be. I feel like Dr. McCroskey has given me the Hope diamond. I know if You gave him the generous spirit to offer me such a rare and wonderful opportunity, I must take it. Please help me do it. Don't let me let him down.

"I'm intrigued, Dr. McCroskey. I don't know if I can write such a project or not, but I'm willing to try."

"Good. I think you'll have fun with it."

A few weeks later I faced a large faculty committee in the Division of Teacher Education at Emory University to make my second project proposal. Dr. McCroskey seemed very excited, and I couldn't understand why. The last time I'd been in front of these men, it had been a dull, routine session. I was in for a shock.

Each professor received a written proposal outlining the background, purpose, and procedure for writing a biography of Edith Fitzgerald. They reacted quickly, with indignation bordering on rage. Questions came at me fast and furiously.

"What makes you think you can write a book?"

"Have you studied writing?"

"Do you have the slightest idea what's involved to guarantee accuracy?"

"What background have you for such a project?"

"What do you know about historical research?"

I felt like a criminal with many accusers and one lone voice trying to defend me.

Dr. McCroskey's answers stressed the urgency of the

project. "There is no real record of Miss Fitzgerald's life and work. One or two superficial articles were published after her death. Few of her contemporaries are left, and there are no known relatives. Now is the time to collect the facts available about Miss Fitzgerald, if the world to which she contributed so much is to know her. Any delay may result in losing vital firsthand information."

"How do you know such information is obtainable?" a tall, thin professor asked.

"Mrs. Stewart has made initial contacts. Responses indicate Miss Fitzgerald's few remaining friends and associates are united in the desire to help commemorate her."

Again they all seemed to be screaming protests. "How can she do it, with no training?"

I looked from one man to another in horror. These were the men I'd respected so much. I'd even been intimidated by some of them. Why they were small, mean, and maybe crazy.

Father, why are they so threatened? You'd think I was doing something to them. They're so emotional. Why?

Then I observed Dr. Ladd, the head of the entire education department. He hadn't spoken. I'd not noticed him before because his small figure had been obscured as the other professors left their seats, striding and pacing in excitement. Suddenly I felt truly shaken. Dr. Ladd had a grin on his face, as if amused by an unshared joke. Maybe it was me.

When Dr. Ladd spoke, a hush came over the professors. His brilliance as well as his position commanded respect. "Mrs. Stewart, would you mind leaving the room?"

My face must have shown shocked disbelief, for Dr. McCroskey hurried to my chair, helped me rise, and escorted me to the next room.

"Don't worry," Dr. McCroskey said hurriedly and turned back.

"I'll pray," I said to myself. "You go back to the lion's den."

Father, it isn't the project they object to, is it? It is me. Thank You that Dr. McCroskey will fight for me. Help him.

A long time passed before Dr. McCroskey came for me. "Mrs. Stewart, please come with me."

I searched his face for a clue but couldn't tell anything. When we entered the room, the change was tremendous. Each professor sat in dignified contrast to the last scene. I'd never forget seeing them on their feet, yelling, while one professor actually threw my proposal on the floor! Now order reigned.

Lord, it appears the jury's in.

"After deliberating, Mrs. Stewart, it has been decided to accept your proposal—with three conditions," Dr. Ladd announced.

My relief was so great over hearing "accept" that I almost missed hearing the three conditions.

"You will take the necessary steps to develop your competence in historical research techniques," Dr. Ladd stated.

Oh, Lord, what on earth does that mean?

"You will secure the advice and assistance of a faculty member in the history department, and this person will be asked to serve on the project committee."

Lord, that's great. Miss Rogers will have to go. Maybe I'll get some real help.

Dr. Ladd grinned again, and I wondered what the third proviso would be.

"I will be added to your committee, Mrs. Stewart." His eyes twinkled.

Oh, Lord, Dr. Ladd on my committee? This must be a very important project. How can I do it? Oh, please help me.

The silence that followed made me feel time had stopped. I had the sensation of a dreamer. Nothing could be real. Dr. McCroskey looked at me intently and cleared his throat. I realized something was expected of me. It was all I could do to stand and murmur, "Thank you, gentlemen."

There was no comment as I left the room.

29

Working, Really Working

For the next year I would have several PhDs watching my work closely.

A bulletin from Dr. McCroskey stated that I would no longer be under Miss Rogers' clinical supervision, but would report directly to him. Dr. McCroskey served as my project adviser. Miss Rogers was removed from my Orals Committee and Dr. Ladd was added. I was allowed to select one other member from any school of higher learning, and I requested Dr. Manford George Gutzke, Professor of Bible at Columbia Seminary. Dr. Duncan, of Emory's History Department, played the most important part in the development of my project. I would meet with him every few weeks for criticism and advice. He was the person who could help me meet the first two provisos for the faculty's approval.

Tuition money for the summer quarter came from my step-grandmother. She sent a check for three hundred dollars along with a very encouraging note. Usually I only heard from her at Christmas time when she sent a card and a small check "With love to each dear one."

In the summer I had a full load of clinical cases and worked in the diagnostic clinic as well. It was the equivalent of "student teaching." I applied for work with the Atlanta Public Schools. Mr. Brown, assistant personnel director, virtually assured me of a position and gave me some sound advice.

"Work hard and get that degree this year!" he urged. "You will be tempted to let it slip by you. The pressures of a new job will demand so much of your attention that you may put off work on your thesis. You'll have five schools to serve. That is a lot of faculties and students to know. You'll have orientation meetings, P.T.A. meetings, and faculty meetings, afternoon and night. It could be easy for you to postpone work on your master's, but don't! Each year that passed would make it harder to meet the requirements. This is the best time—while you are close. Set your goal to graduate in June of 1964 and meet it!"

In August I reported to my new job, thinking academic requirements had been met. Unfortunately, I failed the comprehensive so Dr. Ladd insisted I take five hours in Educational Psychology. Another hundred and fifty dollars! Current bills were piling up again, too. I went to a bank to borrow three hundred. Much to my surprise, it was easy. I had a job!

The need for money and the thought of holding my first check for a moment made me count the days until payday! When it finally came, I learned that new teachers weren't included on that payroll. My first check arrived the following payday, and it was disappointing. Deductions were made for taxes, pension, and insurance. It seemed insufficient to pay creditors as much as I wanted to and still live.

I needed a car for my job as itinerant speech therapist. I was able to buy a little Rambler for $100 down (given by a friend) and small monthly payments.

Dr. McCroskey called me. "How would you like to start a program in tongue thrust therapy at the Speech School?"

Lord, how wonderful You are to provide help when I'd never have dreamed of asking for another job!

"I'd like it very much if it pays."

"Come over and let's discuss it. I don't know how much you learned in this field, but a group of orthodontists want us to hold classes. They asked that you teach it."

After we made terms, I told Jerry, my audiologist friend, about the proposition.

"I'm going to do it, Jerry, but it won't help me financially as much as I'd hoped. I'll have to hire a baby-sitter while I teach the night classes. That cuts the profit, but I feel it will be worth it to gain the experience."

"I'll stay with the children on Monday nights for you," Jerry offered.

"Why. Jerry, what a generous thing to do."

"I won't mind a bit. Sue and Sydney are very dear to me, after all our musical evenings together. Hunt is no trouble. They go to bed early, and I have plenty of work I can bring with me."

This made it possible for me to earn the entire amount, and I liked the idea of being on the Speech School staff. Even part-time, I thought, added prestige.

The biggest morale booster on my thesis came by way of a package containing original letters from Edith Fitzgerald to Marie Kinnard. This source material was quite a surprise because Mrs. Kinnard hadn't told me about the letters when I'd visited her at the Georgia State School for the Deaf. The letters were very personal. It took many weeks for Mrs. Kinnard to decide I could be trusted with the precious contents.

I carried the letters with me to the Emory campus the day I was to register for the late afternoon class in Educational Psychology. The class had already been filled by earlier applicants. When refused admittance, I reported to Dr. McCroskey's campus office and told him my latest problem.

"Why didn't you get here earlier?" he demanded.

"I came as soon as I got off work."

"This is the only time it's offered. If you don't get in this class, you can't graduate in June. You'll have to wait until August, or after next fall."

"I didn't know. Can't you do something? I must finish in June," I pleaded.

"Wait here, I'll go talk to Dr. Ladd."

While he was gone, I entertained myself by reading Miss Fitzgerald's letters. They were filled with feeling. My biography would have been nothing without these documents. The information would bring it to life. I could sense Edith Fitzgerald's suffering. She'd worried about jobs as much as I had!

Dr. McCroskey looked dejected when he returned. "I'm sorry, Suzanne. There's nothing I can do. The class is closed."

I felt so sorry for him! If only I'd known the matter was so important, perhaps I could have taken the morning off to register. Maybe sharing my good news would help lift his spirits.

"Well, I'll graduate someday. That's the main thing. Look what came in the mail! Mrs. Kinnard sent me a collection of letters from Miss Fitzgerald."

"What? Let me see." Excitedly, he read one, then another.

Elated that he shared my enthusiasm, I said, "But look at *this* one."

Suddenly he scooped up all the letters and bolted for the door. "Just wait," he called over his shoulder, "I'll be back. I must show these to Dr. Ladd."

When he returned with a broad grin on his tanned face, I knew something wonderful had happened.

"Here, Mrs. Stewart, go and register!"
He handed me a memo from Dr. Ladd.

Suzanne Stewart has permission to register for Education 210,
even if this means passing the enrollment limit.
                                                        Edward T. Ladd, Ph.D.

In September of 1963 I began my professional work in
two jobs, took a course at Emory, and continued research
and writing of Edith Fitzgerald's life. Somehow the children and I managed to have a fairly normal home life,
along with church and choir attendance. We celebrated
birthdays and special occasions and loved each other and
our friends.

It was a common occurence to find a note in my mailbox at the Speech School saying, "See me. RLM." Usually
the summons was for the purpose of discussing one of my
clinical reports, a particular patient, or review of my thesis.
At the end of one of these conferences, Dr. McCroskey
spoke casually just as I rose to leave.

"By the way, we're having Layman's Day at St. Mark's
on October 20th. They've asked me to do the sermon. I
thought you might be interested."

Was I! Thrills ran through me. "That's wonderful. I'd
like very much to come."

"I thought you might," his sheepish smile told me he
was pleased at my reaction.

"Yes, of course. I'll be there!" Did he remember the
conversation about his former minister that we had had
a year before?

In November the school system gave me time off to
attend the American Speech and Hearing Association
National Convention in Chicago. Though expensive, I
decided to go because I'd discovered Miss Fitzgerald had

relatives living near there. We had corresponded, but personal interviews would help me much more with the book.

Before I left, my friend, Marilyn Munson, invited me over for a special reason. I always accepted her invitations with pleasure. She delighted her guests with a cheerful atmosphere, good food, and loving concern for their interests.

"Come in and see what I have for you!" she greeted me at the door.

Just to look at her made me feel good. Marilyn had a round, serene face, lovely skin, with eyes and lips that broke into laughter at every opportunity. She possessed prettiness and poise that made you feel she'd never had a care in the world.

She led me to the guest bedroom and gestured to a wardrobe of beautiful clothes lying on the twin beds.

"For me?" I gasped excitedly.

"All you want. I've gained weight but refused to admit I wouldn't go back to size six again. I think the Lord wanted them saved for you. You might need them in Chicago."

The trip benefited me in many ways. Just the change of scene helped, diverting my thoughts from the numerous responsibilities in my life. I returned home refreshed.

December. January. February. Before I knew it, spring of 1964 arrived.

Edie Bovee solved the biggest problem concerning my thesis.

"Edie, I'm having a terrible time trying to type the biography. It's hard enough to write it. Emory University doesn't care if I hire someone to type the manuscript, but I can't find anyone who knows how to meet the specifications about footnotes and spacing. The typing has to be accurate."

"I know. I typed Chuck's and mine when we worked on our master's. I did Chuck's dissertation for his doctorate, too. I'll do yours."

She refused to take any money.

"No," she said firmly. "I know what you're up against. Chuck and I have been through it."

We worked together on Sunday afternoons. After church I'd bring fried chicken and Edie would have the rest of dinner prepared. We'd eat with all our children, then work while they played.

Taking the comprehensive loomed over my head like a dark cloud. The reason it was difficult for speech and hearing people was because it was not specifically in our field. The majority of our graduate work was specialized, while the required comprehensive covered six subjects: educational philosophy, psychology, history, curriculum, sociology, and statistics.

Long before, during the first quarter at Emory, I'd been impressed by two women in one of my classes. Mrs. Joyner and Mrs. Geren were teachers who were working on six-year certificates. Providentially, both taught in two of the schools in which I now worked. When I asked them to help me prepare for the crucial exam, they gladly agreed.

March. April. May.

The deadline for everything was the last week in May. Would I make it?

30

Reactions

"Oh, Edie, I've never been so proud of anything in my life. It's perfect!" I cried as I clutched the manuscript Edie had just finished typing.

"Don't feel too good. After you turn it in, your committee will find plenty to correct," Edie answered without emotion.

"I can't believe they'd find fault. Why, there's not a typographical error in it. You've done a remarkable job." Why couldn't Edie share my happiness? I wondered. She'd made my thesis into a work of art with her beautiful typing. I wanted her to be proud of it, too.

"Believe me, when you get it back there will be editorial markings all over it," she stated matter-of-factly.

"But, Edie, Dr. Duncan approved and complimented me on the text. Your typescript couldn't be better. Dr. McCroskey and Dr. Ladd will love it. I think they'll accept it."

"Suzanne, the Director of Education is bound to find fault with it," she persisted.

"I don't see how he can. There isn't a mistake in it," I wasn't being stubborn—just my usual naïve self.

"That's what you think now. After they edit it, you'll have to rewrite, and I'll have to type another version."

"There isn't much time," I said, shocked.

"I know. You *must* be ready to make the corrections and any other demands. I'll need an electric typewriter for speed. They rent them at office supply companies."

Oh, Lord, You know I don't want them to do that! Please make them accept this version.

So many of my prayers had been answered as asked that I fully expected this one to be. And, though I appreciated Edie's earnestness, I thought her pessimistic. Realistic would have been more accurate.

Excitedly, I personally delivered copies to Dr. Gutzke, Dr. McCroskey, and Dr. Ladd. Each promised to read and return my thesis quickly. I looked forward to their praise.

Dr. Gutzke returned his and said, "You've done a remarkable work, Suzanne. I don't know anything about the technicalities of a hearing problem, or didn't until I read this thesis. It is a very interesting manuscript!"

I basked in the glory of his kind words.

Dr. McCroskey's manuscript was returned with a note that brought tears of joy to my eyes.

Suzanne,
   I am very pleased with this document. I think you have produced one of our better master's projects.
   I have dictated at length on *suggested* editorial changes, but there is no real criticism of the substance of the work. You've done an excellent job of letting me meet Edith Fitzgerald.

                                                             RLM

Then I picked up Dr. Ladd's. I couldn't believe it! The black marks of his editing pencil were all through the manuscript. He'd even changed the table of contents. There were notes in the margin, such as, "You must give sources for *all* your information all the way through."

"Is this really germane to your story?" "Not clear what you mean." "How do you know how they feel? All you can say with certainty is how they *say* they feel." "Put this in footnote, otherwise you're jumping the reader ahead of your story." One time he wrote "Abridge to about a sentence." The passage he'd marked was twenty-two lines long!

Dr. Ladd struck through "Miss Fitzgerald" dozens of times, substituting "Edith," and there were many verb tense changes.

Now I knew what Edie had been trying to tell me. I felt like throwing the book in the trash and giving up. Dr. Ladd is unreasonable, I thought angrily. No one could rewrite in the little time left and get it typed. It was impossible.

"You must," the inner voice said.

Somehow I made the corrections in a few days, discussed the revision with Dr. Ladd, and delivered the thesis to Edie. I hoped she could get the job done. I had to study and continue going to work each day.

While working with a little boy who stuttered, I received a jolt.

"MMMMMMrs. Stewart, why is your eye bbbbbbbleeding?" he asked.

"Don't be silly, Jeff. Now go on with your reading."

"BBBBBBBBut your eye is bbbbbbbleeding," he insisted.

"It couldn't be. I don't feel anything."

"BBBBBBBBut it is! Look in the mmmmmirror."

To humor him and get on with the lesson, I did. Shocked, I saw that the white area was filled with blood.

When Dr. Jackson looked at it later that day, he said, "It is caused by a strained blood vessel. You've overworked your eyes since going to graduate school. They're five years older than you are! You must slow down. Rest them."

"I can't now. I have to study for the comprehensive this Saturday."

What if I go blind? I thought.

"Use good sense," Dr. Jackson warned. "Give them a little relief from time to time. Rest them every half hour. Study twenty-eight minutes, then close your eyes and relax for two minutes."

When I entered the air-conditioned room on the Emory campus Saturday morning, I prayed my last prayer about the comprehensive exam.

Lord, please help. I've done everything I know to do. I've studied to the best of my ability. Please keep my mind clear and able to recall what I've learned. Let me pass if it be Thy will.

The pressure of the exam was partially due to time. I hurried to finish each section, yet never had time to double-check my answers. When the ordeal ended, my whole body ached. I looked in a mirror to see if my eye was bleeding again. No.

Thank You, Lord. I couldn't take time to rest them.

I drove to Edie and Chuck's house. Edie sat at the typewriter working diligently on my thesis.

"You might just as well stop, Edie. I failed the comprehensive," I stated dramatically.

She stopped only for a moment. "How do you know?" she asked.

"I just know," I muttered gloomily. "It was harder than last time. I couldn't possibly have passed."

She resumed typing. "That doesn't mean anything. Naturally you feel like you failed. It's just a reaction."

"No," I insisted, "I know I failed. I left lots of questions blank."

She didn't answer. The only sound was the fast clicking of the keys.

"Where are the children?"

"Chuck took them on a picnic so I could work in peace."

"You're killing yourself for a lost cause. I've let you down."

Impatiently Edie spoke to me, "This has to be ready Monday. No matter what happened today, the deadline for this is Monday. I'm running out of time, and you're not helping. I couldn't be this far along except Marilyn brought her maid over to take care of the children and the house yesterday, and Chuck is helping this weekend."

"Marilyn did that? That was nice of her." I felt guilty, knowing how hard my friends were pulling for me. Later Marilyn told me more of the problems that came during those days. The paper I'd supplied ran out. Chuck told Edie not to disturb me about it while I was preparing for the exam. Edie used her grocery money to buy the good bond paper needed. The Bovees got through those days on peanut butter sandwiches and little else.

"Edie, I could just die. I've let everybody down. *Why?* Other Christians I've known come through with top honors. *How can you go on typing calmly when I have failed so miserably?*"

"I'm not calm. I'm very nervous, and you're making me more nervous," she rose and started pushing me toward the door. "If I make a mistake on a page, I have to do it over. It takes a lot of time to put carbon paper between six sheets and line it up. I haven't got time to make mistakes, and I will if you stay here. I don't know if you failed the exam or not. I hope not. But it doesn't affect this. My job is to do the thesis. It is going to be ready

Monday if I have to kick you out. You'll just have to go somewhere else now and leave me alone. I haven't got time to pacify you."

I knew she was right and admired the strength she showed. Still, I was hurt and confused from the long tests and needed comfort. I went to the Gutzke's.

Mrs. Gutzke opened the door and sensed my need immediately. She put her arm around me and led me to the porch. I must have looked very forlorn. "I'll call Manford. He's having a little nap, but he'll be right out. You sit in the rocker and I'll bring you some tea. Just a minute."

Oh, Lord, these people are so good. How could I fail?

I wept while waiting, but when Dr. Gutzke joined me, I started ranting. "Edie is working her fingers to the bone typing my thesis, and it doesn't matter. I'm not going to graduate. I failed the comprehensive today. How could I?"

"I doubt you did. You're being too hard on yourself."

"But I did!"

"No, you passed," he said with a benign smile.

"Oh, Dr. Gutzke, you're wrong. That's what is hurting me so badly. You believe in me. So does Dr. Broyles. All my friends have tried so hard to help me, and I'm not worth it. I just don't have what it takes. For two years I've had everyone I could get praying for me, and now this. *I'll never ask anyone to pray for me again.*"

"What do you think got you through this far?"

"But what good is it if I failed?"

"But you didn't."

"How can you know that? *I* took the exam."

"I know because you're like the church in Philadelphia. You have 'a little strength.'"

"You're comparing me with the church in Revelation?"

"Yes. Chapter 3. No man can shut the door God opened for you. You will graduate."

I left his home subdued, but not convinced. I still felt low.

Dear Lord, I don't want to go home. I can't face the children yet. But I won't bother any more of my friends. Help me get my mind off myself. Where can I go?

"Why don't you buy a hat?"

I almost laughed aloud at the thought. I couldn't afford one, of course. But why not? I hadn't done anything reckless in a long time.

The big event in Atlanta that week was a visit from President Lyndon B. Johnson. He had addressed a group of Georgia legislators at an integrated breakfast the day before. With history in the making, I had missed the parades and excitement because of my personal responsibility. Well, I was through. The exam was over. I'd celebrate. I'd search until I found a straw hat styled like a Texas cowboy's!

When I found one that answered that description and made me feel good, I cocked it to one side of my head and winked at my reflection in the mirror.

Thank you, Father. I'll love this hat forever.

31

All Over Now!

On Monday, after working in two schools until three o'clock, I picked up the copies of my thesis. Edie had completed typing it on schedule. There was one copy for the Emory Teacher Education Library, one for the library of the Atlanta Speech School, one for Dr. Mc-Croskey's personal library, one for Miss Fitzgerald's family, and two for me. I delivered them to Dr. McCroskey's box at the Atlanta Speech School, rushed home to have dinner with the children, and returned to the Speech School to teach my night classes.

Dr. McCroskey was sitting at the reception desk in the lobby when I arrived. He signed the six copies of my thesis as I watched.

"Approved for submission to the division, May 11, 1964," he read. "Now they're ready for Dr. Ladd's signature."

"You think he will approve?"

"Yes. It is a wonderful document. It should inspire many young teachers."

"Dr. McCroskey, do you know if I passed the comprehensive?"

"It's close. I've talked to Sarah, the secretary, in Teacher Education. She said five of the six categories are in.

You're okay so far, but you have to score well in the last one."

"What is it?"

"Educational Psychology."

I groaned. Then shrugged and said, "Well, if I can't get a degree this way, I'll just have to wait for an honorary!"

Dr. McCroskey smiled slowly and said appreciatively, "Mrs. Stewart, I like your spirit!"

"And I like yours." Waving, I rushed up the steps to my classroom.

An hour later when I came down the steps, Dr. McCroskey was ending a telephone conversation. I could see his lips moving. "Thanks, Sarah."

I paused at the foot of the staircase, feeling almost paralyzed. He knew the results, and I was about to hear. Could I take it? He walked toward me. It seemed a minute a step. Why didn't he speak. About ten feet away, he grinned.

"You made it. You passed. My congratulations, Mrs. Stewart." He bowed.

Overcome with gratitude and humility, I whispered, "I don't deserve it."

Erect, he dropped his mockery and turned steps into strides. "Oh, yes, you do!" he spoke emphatically. "They didn't give you a thing. You earned every bit of it!"

"I must tell mother."

"First call Dr. Gutzke. The orals are scheduled for tomorrow at four o'clock. See if that is convenient for him. Can you get there by then?"

The next day Dr. Gutzke and I arrived at the same time, and I called to him as I parked by Emory's educational building. "Hi! Wait for me."

He took my arm as we walked toward the building. "Well, girl, how did you sleep?"

"Beautifully. I've never been so happy."

"No fears?"

"None. I'm not afraid of orals. Never have been. I can express myself better verbally than on paper. I'm so glad *you're* here, though. If I get in trouble, you help me out."

"Do you expect them to give you a hard time?"

"I don't know. Maybe. I know other students who've failed their orals, but I just can't worry about it. I've been through the worst. I know you and Dr. McCroskey are on my side. That's a majority, though I'd like to pass with a unanimous decision of my committee, even if no one knows it is on the records but me."

He squeezed my hand as we entered Dr. Ladd's office. The three men greeted each other cordially, excused themselves, and entered Dr. Ladd's private office, leaving me alone. The secretary had gone for the day.

Thank You, Lord, that I do not feel alone. I'm relaxed. If there is any chance of failure now, I don't feel it. You've brought me this far. Be with me now.

Soon I was called in and the questions began. I found them interesting and enjoyed expressing myself. It was the first time I'd ever felt at ease under pressure. Then Dr. Ladd asked a strange question.

"Mrs. Stewart, are you a scholar?"

Lord, now I need help! How am I supposed to answer that? If I say "Yes," he'll think me presumptuous. If I say "No," why should he let me graduate?

I looked at Dr. Gutzke, then at Dr. McCroskey. No suggestion of a smile from either. I met Dr. Ladd's glinting eyes. "Well, I'm not a professional scholar," I answered.

He made no comment and questions concerning my field of specialization were resumed.

Shortly after, Dr. Ladd pushed back his chair, announcing, "I think that is enough, gentlemen. Mrs. Stewart will you wait in the other office a few minutes?"

This is the last time I'll ever have to "wait outside," I thought, satisfied.

Soon the door opened and they filed out, all looking very pleased.

Dr. Ladd took my hand, "Congratulations, Mrs. Stewart. We're proud to have you graduate from our department. I hope you will allow your book to be published."

Dr. Gutzke's eyes twinkled. "Good girl. You know your material. Congratulations."

Lastly, my dear friend and champion, Dr. McCroskey, took my hand. "Congratulations, Mrs. Stewart. You are *indeed* a scholar!"

32

Commencement Means Beginning

"MAMA, WHY CAN'T we go with you?" my little Sydney asked coquettishly.

"You'd have such a long time to wait, honey, and the sun might be too hot. Mother Sue will bring you in time to get a good seat."

"Why are you leaving now, mama?"

"The graduates have to get dressed. Everyone wears a long, black robe, but some of us get to wear a hood because we're getting a higher degree." I smiled just thinking about it.

"What color, mama?" Sue asked.

"They have different colors. Mine is light blue trimmed in blue velvet. That's for Arts and Sciences. It is lined in purple and gold—Emory's colors."

Later I realized they probably visualized me as "Red Riding Hood" and might be disappointed.

"Good-by, darlings. Mother Sue is coming up the driveway. I must go now."

All three huddled around me, hugging and kissing.

"Have a good time, mama."

"I will. I'll see you there, and tomorrow we'll go to Montreat!"

Marilyn Munson had offered me the use of her home at Montreat, North Carolina, for a vacation. The children loved it there and were looking forward to the trip.

Driving to Emory, I thought of all the nice things that had happened. A telegram had come that morning from my Sunday school teacher, and I'd received notes and cards from other well-wishers.

Chuckling, I recalled a cartoon sent anonymously:

> Use me, Lord! Use me!
> I'll go anywhere
> —do anything
> Suffer abject poverty,
> make any sacrifice . . .
> even martyrdom.
> Well, studying wasn't
> exactly what I had in mind.

I felt happy, relaxed, good! I didn't mind waiting in line at the university or standing for long periods of time. Everything seemed glorious.

I saw a long, long row of people in colorfully hooded robes and exclaimed to the medical student next to me, "Why, that must be the whole faculty!"

"Yes, it is. We walk by them for congratulations."

"We speak to each one?"

"If you want to. They're here to shake your hand."

My heart started beating faster. How wonderful! These men and women, though mostly strangers to me, understood the meaning of our accomplishment in a way even family and friends did not. How grand to have each one's personal good wishes.

The late afternoon couldn't have been more beautiful. The sun shone but wasn't uncomfortably hot. The green of the grounds and the blue sky framed the university quadrangle with majesty. It was a beautiful sight.

Oh, thank You, Father, that it didn't rain.

I could hear the organist playing the *Choral Prelude*.
When it ended, the Processional began, and we started
moving slowly to Marcello's *Psalms XX.*

*Oh, Father, how appropriate. You heard me in
trouble, helped and strengthened, and answered my
prayers. I am glad that You are honored now.*

The impressive and lengthy procession was led by the
marshalls of the university followed by the candidates for
degrees, faculties, administrative officers, candidates for
honorary degrees, the chairman of the Board of Trustees,
and the president of the university.

Many of the restless students were glad to be moving.
I'd heard them complaining while we'd waited. All the
procedure thrilled me! A strange contrast to those who
were bored, looking on this as just another hot, dull night
in June. I understood. I'd not gone to my own college
graduation years before, but had had the diploma mailed.
There is quite a difference when you struggle and work
toward a prized goal. Every step I took made me that
much more grateful to be a part of the proceedings.

*Thank You, Father, for making me appreciative, at
last. Forgive me for taking my privileges for granted
when I was young. Thank You for my mother and
the patient people who cared for me when I was so
selfish.*

As the conferring of degrees began, I glanced over
my shoulder. Mom, my aunt Janie, Sue, Sydney, and
Hunt all sat on the front row of the guests' section.
Further over I saw Rosemary Joyce, and Lettie.

Excitement mounted as each row of students went forward. Finally the graduates in my row stood and moved down the aisle toward the rostrum. My heart pounded, and then I heard my name. Never before had it been spoken so majestically or loudly! It seemed to permeate the atmosphere and ring against the stillness as I walked across the stage. I felt twelve feet tall as I shook hands and received that sought-after piece of paper that elevated me to a world of recognized service to mankind. A special sensation went through me as President Atwood took my hand.

Happier than I'd ever been in my life, I stepped down to the opposite aisle to be met by my little boy. He'd run down front, unable to sit still. Smiling brightly, Hunt took my hand and shared my moment of triumph. I squeezed his hand and grinned. His small feet had to skip to keep up with me as I walked briskly back to my row. Then I gave him a quick hug, kiss, and my degree. "Take it to Mother Sue," I whispered.

My feeling of elation didn't diminish as I disrobed and left the campus for Rosemary's house. She and Pete were giving me a party, and I could hear mother playing the piano as I arrived. Joyce and Kent were there, along with Jerry, Lettie, Dr. and Mrs. Gutzke, and Marilyn and Don Munson. What a happy group of precious people! They all hugged me when I entered.

"Suzy, if you had it to do over, would you?" Kent asked.

"You bet! I'd have gone through anything to have the feelings I have right now."

"Is it better than your wedding day?" Joyce asked.

"Yes. Better than anything I've ever experienced in my life."

"That's because you did this all by yourself," Rosemary said gaily.

"By *myself?* Why, God used thousands of people to help me," I answered seriously.

"Yes, but you *still* did it alone. When you marry or have babies, someone else is involved. This was strictly between you and God."

"It is very personal. But the joy of it is in sharing with all of you."

"Open your gifts," Rosemary gestured to a table. "Doris brought this before she and Frank left for his eastern tour."

I read the note aloud.

> Dearest Suzanne,
>   This is a wee gift to keep you cool and pretty this summer. We are so proud of you all the time, but especially today when your sleepless nights and "mountains of prayers" carried you down for your master's degree and a special place in the field of education. We know you were sustained and the victor only through Him who gave you that Eternal Diploma a few years ago. The world is yours!
>
>   Much love,
>   Doris and Frank

"Oh, look," I gasped, unwrapping a beautiful dress. "How sweet."

There was a book from Dr. and Mrs. Gutzke, a record album from Jerry, a gold pin from the Munsons, a gold fountain pen and pencil set from Janie, and a card full of money from Lettie, Rosemary, and Joyce.

"This will really make my vacation!" I said happily.

We sat around in a circle and each person told something he or she especially remembered. Dr. Gutzke entertained us with his version of my orals.

Pete said, "I really was worried about this gal, and told Rosemary so. 'Invite her over and let's see if she's all right.' Well, she told Rosemary she was going somewhere but would stop by to say 'Hi.' When I opened the door, she stood there in a three-hundred dollar dress someone had given her, her hair styled out of this world, and said she was on her way to the opera. I told Rosemary then I'd never worry about her again!"

We laughed and we cried.

Jerry said, "I can't help remembering at this moment that the real meaning of 'commencement' is 'beginning.' " I thought of that on the way home and as I went to sleep.

Lord, thank You for being with me now and all my life.

The next day I telephoned Rosemary. "I just wanted to thank you again before we left for Montreat. The party was marvelous."

Her rippling laughter came quickly. "It certainly was your night! I've never seen anyone so completely the center of attention as you were!"

"Yes. Everyone was wonderful to me. I'll never forget it."

"Are you still walking on clouds today?"

"I'm very happy. Last night I was in sort of a daze. Today I feel normal but still have a glow on!"

"Suzanne, I don't think any of us have ever seen God working in a person's life as clearly as in yours. Your graduation touched me deeply. It was a miracle—the best of many miracles."

"I know. From the time I decided to take God's word literally and believe everything Jesus said, I knew He *could* take care of us, but I didn't know how He *would*."

"You must feel relieved of much pressure."

"I do. I have a sense of well-being that is unbelievable. I have a sense of absolute freedom."

"Is that the main change?"

I thought a minute. "No, I guess not. I've had the assurance God loves me, and now others can see it. But He's given me something I never had before, and didn't know I was receiving until graduation was certain."

"What?" Rosemary asked softly but eagerly.

"He's given me self-respect. Rosemary, no one will ever know how inadequate I've felt most all my life. I never did anything worthwhile and was too weak to change. I was completely dependent on other people, particularly mother and John. Why, I didn't even like to drive a car!"

"I know," she said quietly.

"God did for me what I couldn't do for myself. He changed me from an inadequate person, filled with shame and guilt because I was spoiled and felt inferior, to a contributing person. It's not just that I can make a living for the children, though that's fantastic. It's that now I can really do some good in this world. My life will not be a total loss.

"The person I used to be doesn't even exist, except in memory. God has given me a new life."

Rosemary didn't answer, and I knew she was weeping. In joy.

"Well, I must hang up now. The children are anxious to start on our trip."

"Have a *good* time!" she managed to say cheerfully, though her voice cracked.

Yes, Lord, the good time, the best time is ahead of us. You've proved to me that the future is always better than the past—with You! This knowledge is what I want to spend the rest of my life sharing with others. Please, let me.